MASERATI
POST WAR BROCHURES THROUGH INLINE 6 CYLINDER CARS

BY

HILARY A. RAAB, JR.

PUBLISHED
BY
VELOCEPRESS

Copyright 2004

VelocePress, an imprint of TheValueGuide, Inc. Reno, Nevada 89509 USA
All rights reserved.

ISBN: 1-58850-045-4

All rights reserved. This work may not be reproduced or transmitted in any form without express written consent of the Publisher.

Trademarks used herein are for identification only.

http://www.VelocePress.com

Maserati Post War Brochures through Inline 6 Cylinder Cars

INTRODUCTION

E' con grande piacere che ho aiutato Hilary Raab nel suo sforzo di catalogazione delle pubblicazioni promozionali che la Maserati ha distribuito nel dopoguerra. Ritengo estremamente positivo l'approccio sistematico che sottintende a questa opera: è infatti dai documenti ufficiali che si iniziano a studiare i fatti storici.

Spesso la storia delle Case automobilistiche italiane (e quindi anche della Maserati) è raccontata dagli storici stranieri in modo colorito e folcloristico: dall'esame di questi cataloghi penso che si possa percepire lo sforzo di un Gruppo industriale, attivo contemporaneamente in diversi settori merceologici, teso sempre alla produzione del meglio.

Rivedendo tutti questi stampati saltano all'occhio quelli relativi agli autocarri elettrici e soprattutto quello automobilistico denominato "la Marca che si impone", relativo ai modelli A6 1500, A6GCS e 4CLT/48: ritengo che questo catalogo, il campione indiscusso fra quelli prodotti dalla Maserati, sia, considerando il periodo, uno dei più belli e completi della intera produzione mondiale.

Vedendo questo catalogo, resta il rimpianto di cosa sarebbe potuta diventare la Maserati se la sua attività industriale non fosse stata, prima frenata e poi addirittura bloccata, da dure lotte sindacali e politiche nel periodo tra il 1948 e il 1952.

La Maserati riuscì a superare tutti questi problemi e in seguito a produrre quelle che molti considerano le più belle vetture sport e formula degli Anni Cinquanta; dopo il ritiro dalle competizioni arrivò una gamma completa di vetture granturismo alle quali, a mio avviso, non sono ancora state completamente riconosciute le loro grandi qualità costruttive.

Sono sicuro che quest'opera consentirà una più completa e precisa conoscenza dei prodotti Maserati.
- *Adolfo Orsi*

I was happy to help Hilary Raab in his effort to catalogue the post-war Maserati's brochures. The methodical approach which drives his work is very positive: in fact it is correct to begin the study of any history starting from the official documents.

Often the history of Italian sports car manufacturers (Maserati included) is narrated by foreign historians in a folkloric way: from the examination of these catalogues I believe it is possible to understand the effort of an industrial group, active in the same period in different fields, always devoted to achieve the best possible result, related to the conditions of those hard times.

Skimming thru all the pages a reader will note the importance of the "elettrocarri" catalogues: in the automobile field I like particularly the one denominated "la Marca che si impone" (the Make which wins"), related to the A6 1500, A6GCS and 4CLT/48 models. I consider this one as the champion of all the Maserati brochures and, considering the period, one of the most beautiful and complete of the worldwide production.

Looking at this catalogue, it remains the regret for what Maserati could have become if their activity should have not been first penalised and later even stopped by political and trade unions wars in the 1948-1952 period.

Maserati was able to overcome this difficult time and later produced these sport and formula cars, which are considered the most beautiful of the Fifties: after the withdrawal from the racing activity, Maserati started a complete line of Granturismo cars which have not yet been fully appreciated for their excellent quality.

I am sure that this work will make possible a more complete and precise knowledge of the Maserati products.
- *Adolfo Orsi*

Maserati Post War Brochures through Inline 6 Cylinder Cars

NOTE FROM THE AUTHOR

Maserati, the oldest of the three Modenese sports car manufactures, and is the only one actually located, in Modena. There were a few pre-war brochures, but this book is on the early post war race and Grand Touring cars through the Mistral. The V8 and V6 cars, up to the Biturbo, will be the subject of another book.

Italy makes dream cars. The brochures were originally made to sell dreams, either racing or Grand Touring. Today the brochures are used to document what was made and how it was made. But, it is also a treasure hunt, with something unexpected turning up at unanticipated places and times. Will we ever know all the brochures that were produced, and their reprints and variations? I doubt it. Enclosed in this book, arranged by type, are the ones that we were able to locate over the years.

In 1998 Maserati published a folder on their history and included reprints of many of the brochures. Some of these reprints were marked on the back, "c1998 Archivo Maserati riproduzione anastatica," but many were not marked. As these sets are broken up, it will lead to the confusion as to what is an original and what is a reprint. Also, some of the early brochures were reprinted in Australia in the 1980's. Some of these were marked and some were not, adding to the confusion. I have tried to list the variations and the reprints to watch out for in each brochure description.

The early "blue line" specification sheets were issued as needed, in limited numbers, and others were more widely distributed. There will always be "new" ones discovered, as they could be printed at will. I have seen some as late as Indy models.

Most of these brochures are from the author's collection. Some were "found" at swap meets around Europe. Many were obtained through Peter Coltrin (deceased) and later through his widow Gabriella Santi Coltrin who still finds old rare brochures. Also, Dr. Adolfo Orsi generously provided some of the obscure brochures and these are so indicated.

I have included the MASERATI motorcycle brochures, even though they were not produced by OFFICINE ALFIERI MASERATI S.P.A., but by a "sister" company after the ORSI Empire was divided between family members in 1952. This company had the right to use the MASERATI Name and Badge for spark plugs and batteries only.

The idea for this book was started over 20 years ago with David Robidoux. We did some planning, and made lists of brochures, but never got any further until now.

Whether you use this book to try to complete a brochure collection, to document an individual car or for research, enjoy the world of MASERATI.

I want to expressly thank Dr. Adolfo Orsi for reading this collection and correcting the Italian spellings and the years of the brochures.

- Hilary A. Raab, Jr.

Maserati Post War Brochures through Inline 6 Cylinder Cars

CONTENTS

LAYOUT STYLES	0.0
MACHINE TOOLS	1.0
POSTCARDS	2.0
ELETTROCARRO (ELECTRIC TRUCKS)	3.0
MOTORI MOTONAUTICA (BOAT MOTORS)	4.0
A6 MODELS	5.0
COMPETITION MODELS	6.0
3500GT, 3500GT SPYDER 1957-1964 (TIPO AM101)	7.0
SEBRING 1963-1970 (TIPO AM101)	8.0
MISTRAL 1964-1970 (TIPO AM109)	9.0
FULL LINE BROCHURES	10.0
BROCHURE LITERATURE HOLDERS	11.0
MOTOCICLI-CICLOMOTORI (MOTORCYCLES)	12.0

Maserati Post War Brochures through Inline 6 Cylinder Cars

LAYOUT STYLES

0.0

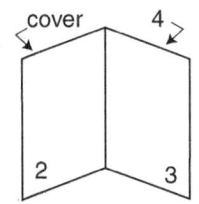
STYLE 1

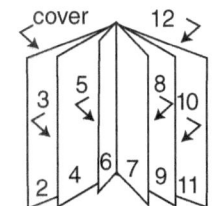
STYLE 6

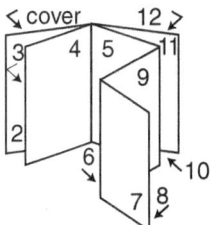
STYLE 12

STYLE 2A

STYLE 7

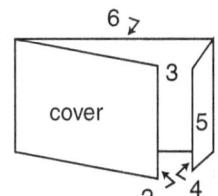
STYLE 13

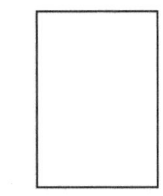
STYLE 2B

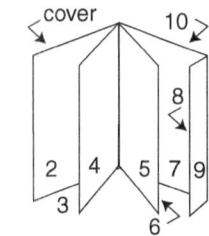
STYLE 8

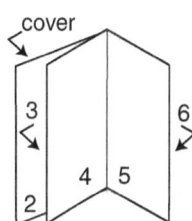
STYLE 14

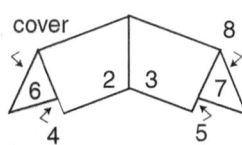
STYLE 3

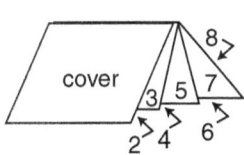
STYLE 9

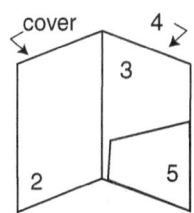
STYLE 15

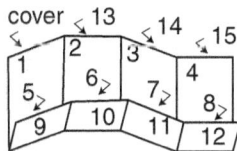
STYLE 4

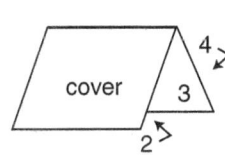
STYLE 10

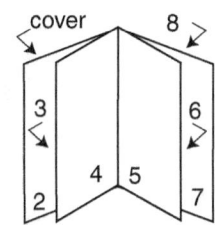
STYLE 5

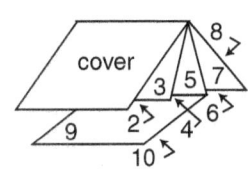
STYLE 11

Chapter Title				Book Section	How the brochure unfolds
Brochure Title					
Type of Brochure	**Size of closed brochure**	**Size of closed brochure**	**Languages**		Style Number

Color = 4 color
Colored = individial colors

" = inches

cm = centimeters

ITA = Italian
ENG = English
FRA = French
DEU = German

Number of reprints or reproductions if different size. Corresponds to number on last page as **"Marked:"**

Descriptions are of Major Colors. Colored pictures with outdoor backgrounds, only colors of the cars are given.

MACHINE TOOLS

1.0

MILLING MACHINES 1-1

THERE WERE ADDITIONAL BROCHURES ON THE MACHINE TOOLS NOT SHOWN HERE. AS THEY BECOME AVAILABLE THEY WILL BE ADDED TO FUTURE EDITIONS OF THIS BOOK.

Machine Tools	section 1-1	
MILLING MACHINES		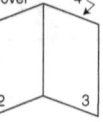
color brochure	11¾ x 8¼"	30 x 21 cm	Italian, French	Style 1

Cover:
Background - green
Print - black
Black and white photo of milling machine

Page 2:
Background - white
Print - black
Top and bottom bands - green

Machine Tools			section 1-1	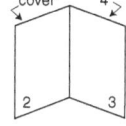
MILLING MACHINES				
color brochure	11³/₄ x 8¹/₄"	30 x 21 cm	Italian, French	Style 1

Page 3:
Background:
    left: green
    right: white
Print - black
Black and white photos

Page 4:
Background - green
Print - black

Marked:
Ufficio Stampa & Propaganda Maserati
Poligafica Bedoniana - Bologna

POSTCARDS

2.0

S.A. FABBRICA CANDELE ACCUMULATORI MASERATI	2-1
FABBRICA CANDELE ACCUMULATORI MASERATI S.P.A.	2-2
MOTO CANDELE ACCUMULATORI	2-3
FABBRICA CANDELE ACCUMULATORI	2-4
MASERATI 1958/1998	2-5
MASERATI MERAK 3000	2-6
MASERATI BORA	2-7

Postcards			section 2-1	
S.A. FABBRICA CANDELE ACCUMULATORI MASERATI				
postcard	6 x 4"	15.2 x 10.4 cm	Italian	Style 2A

NUOVA PRODUZIONE MASERATI
S.A. FABBRICA CANDELE ACCUMULATORI MASERATI

Front:
Background - white
Maserati badge - blue and red
Car - dark red
Uniform and hat - blue
Shoes - brown
Battery - black
Spark plug -   base/black
                   insulator/white
                   cap/yellow
Maserati - red
Print - black

Marked:
STABILIMENTO POLIGRAFICO ARTIOLI - MODENA

Postcards			section 2-2	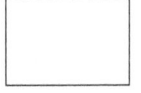	
FABBRICA CANDELE ACCUMULATORI MASERATI S.P.A.					17
postcard	6 x 4"	15.2 x 10.4 cm	Italian	Style 2A	

MASERATI
fabbrica cadele accumulatori Maserati s.p.a.

Front:
Background - white
Maserati badge - blue and red
MASERATI - red with black shadow
Battery - black with green caps and red post
Motorcycle - black with red tank
Man   - left half   green hat
                                   red jacket
                                   blue pants
                                   yellow shoes
             - right half   red helmet
                                   black jacket
                                   black pants
                                   purple shoes
Print - black except fabbrica candele accumulatori
Maserai S.p.A. - blue

Marked:
Litografica Bodoniana - Bologna

18	Postcards		section 2-3	
	MOTO CANDELE ACCUMULATORI			
	postcard	6 x 4" 15.2 x 10.4 cm	Italian	Style 2A

Front:
Background - white
Maserati badge - blue and red
Backgrounds - red, yellow, green and blue
Print - black

Marked:
Litografica Bodoniana - Bologna

Postcards			section 2-4		
FABBRICA CANDELE ACCUMULATORI					19
postcard	4 x 6"	10.6 x 15.2 cm	Italian	Style 2A	

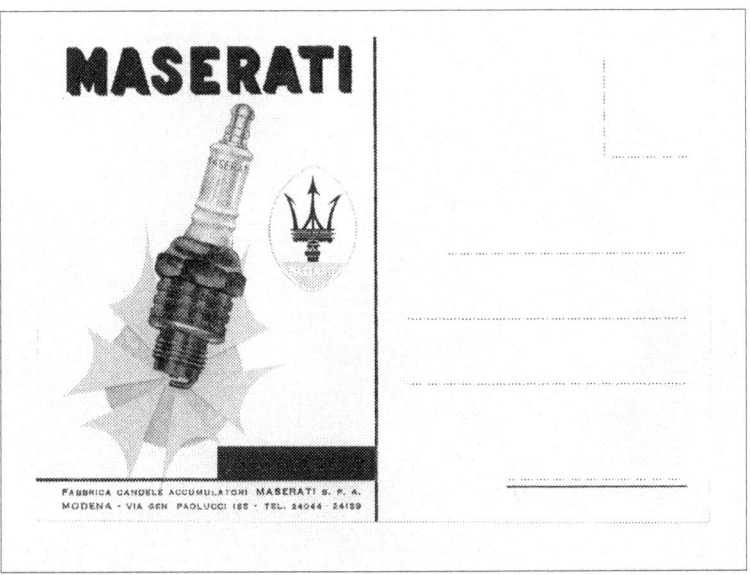

Front:
Background - white
Maserati - red highlighted with black
Maserati badge - blue and red
Spark plug - black base, rose insulator and gold top
Circle - blue with yellow highlights
la candele - black print in red box
Print - black

Rear:
Background - white

Marked:
none

From the collection of Gabriella Coltrin

Postcards			section 2-5	
MASERATI 1958/1998				
postcard	4 x 6"	10.4 x 15.2 cm	Italian	Style 2A

20

Front:
Background - blue
Print and car - silver

Marked:
Artestampa (MO)

Note: not an official factory postcard.

Postcards			section 2-6		
MASERATI MERAK 3000					21
postcard	4 x 6"	10.4 x 15.2 cm	Italian	Style 2A	

Front:
Background - color photo
Car - blue
Walls - white
Floor - brick red

Marked:
Cecami 980

	Postcards			section 2-7	
22	**MASERATI BORA**				
	postcard	4³/₄ x 6³/₄"	12 x 17 cm	Italian	Style 2A

MASERATI BORA
Background - left to right
brown to blue
3/4 car - blue
Car front - yellow
Print - silver

Marked:
ARTI GRAFICHE RICORDI
S.p.A. - Milano

MASERATI ELETTROCARRO

I MODERNI ELETTROCARRI MASERATI 1942	3-1
AUTOCURRO EC 10 TIPO 2 1948	3-2
AUTOCARRO 15 TM - 20 GIUGNO 1951(3-52)	3-3
L'AUTOCARRO UTILITARIO MASERATI "MULETTO"	3-4
AUTOCARRO TM 15 "MULETTO'	3-5
GLI ELETTROMOBILI INDUSTRIALI (REPRINTED)	3-6
GLI AUTOCARRI ELETTRICI MASERATI (REPRINTED)	3-7
AUTOCARRO EC 20	3-8
MASERATI EC.35	3-9
AUTOCARRO EC35	3-10

Maserati Elettrocarro

I MODERNI ELETTROCARRI MASERATI 1942

| black and white sheet | 11½ x 9" | 29.4 x 23.0 cm | Italian | Style 2B |

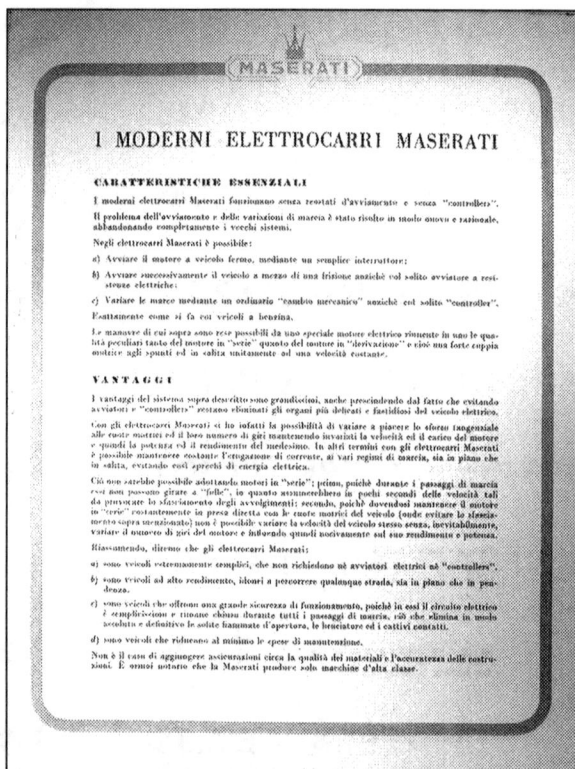

Front:
Background - white
Border and Maserati - gold
Print - black

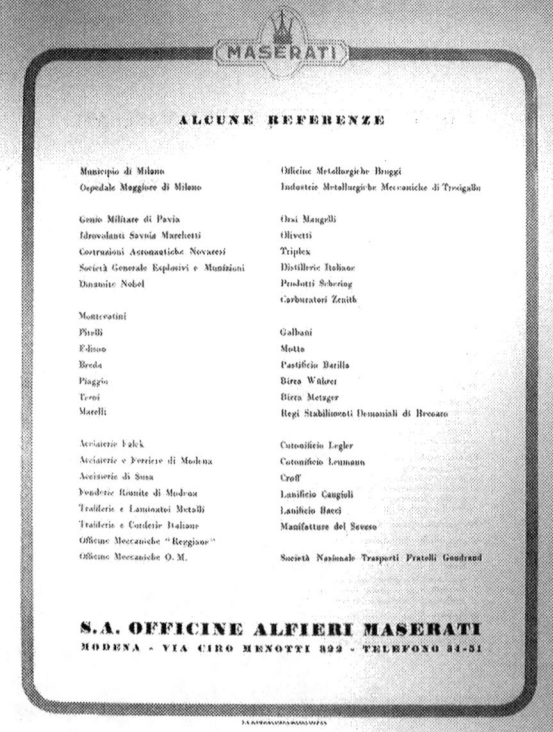

Rear:
Background - white
Border and Maserati - gold
Print - black

Marked:
S.A. ALFERI & LACROIX.MILANO 1942XX

From the collection of Dr. Adolfo Orsi

Maserati Elettrocarro	section 3-2		25

AUTOCARRO EC 10 TIPO 2 1948

| black and white sheet | 11⁷/₁₆ x 8¹/₄" | 29 x 21 cm | Italian | Style 2B |

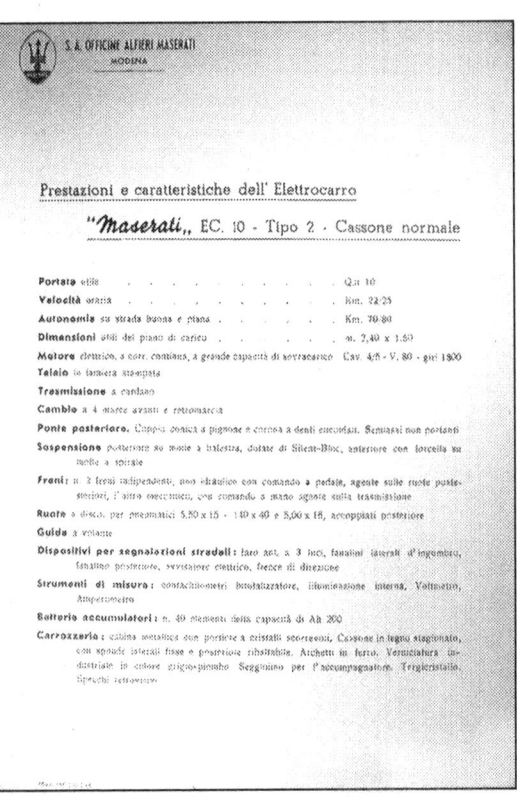

Front:
Background - white
Print - black

Rear:
Background - white
Blank

Marked:
Mod. 169 200 2-48

From the collection of Dr. Adolfo Orsi

26	**Maserati Elettrocarro**		section 3-3	

AUTOCARRO 15 TM - 20 GIUGNO 1951(3-52)

| black and white sheet | 11³/₄ x 8¹/₄" | 30 x 21 cm | Italian | Style 2B |

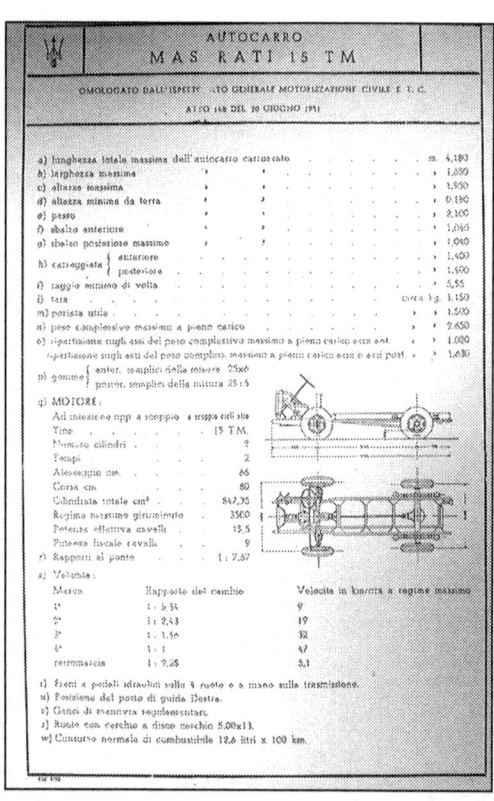

Front:
Background - white
Print - black

Rear:
Background - white
blank

Marked:
450-3-52

Maserati Elettrocarro

L'AUTOCARRO UTILITARIO MASERATI "MULETTO"

| black and white sheet | 11⅝ x 8¼" | 29.5 x 21 cm | Italian | Style 2B |

Front:
Background - brown
Truck - black and white photo
Print - black

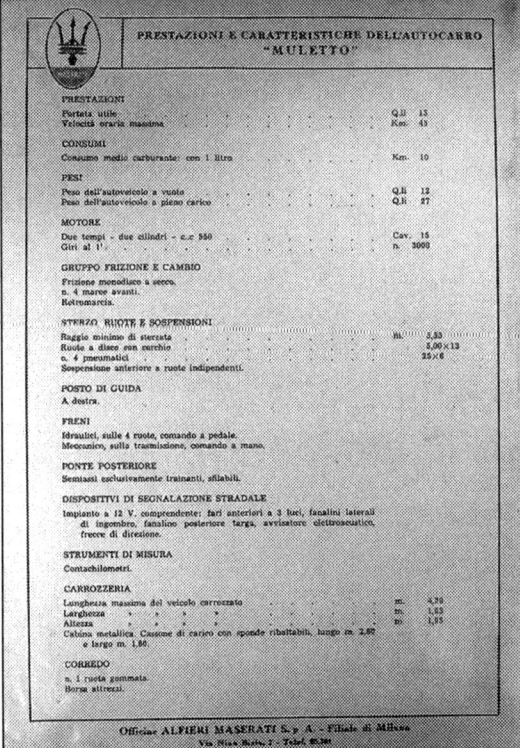

Rear:
Background - white
Print - black

Marked:
none

28	**Maserati Elettrocarro**		section 3-5	
	AUTOCARRO TM 15 "MULETTO"			
	black and white sheet	11³/₄ x 8⁵/₈" · 30 x 21.5 cm	Italian	Style 2B

Front:
Background - white
Truck - black and white photo
Print - black

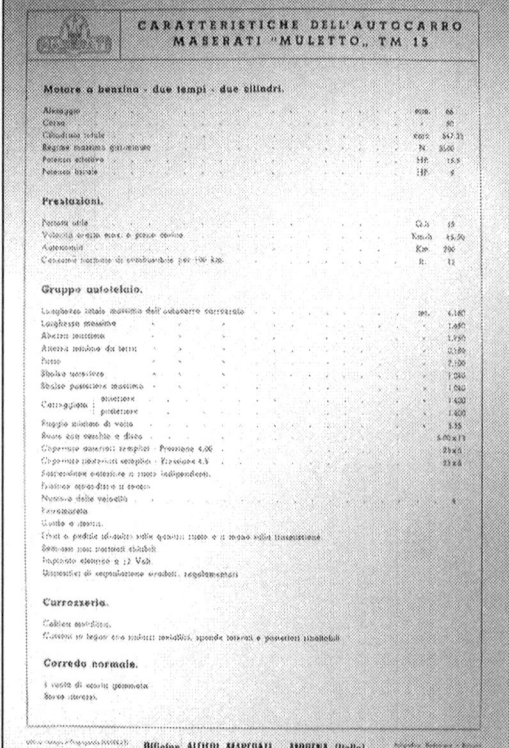

Rear:
Background - white
Print - black

Marked:
Ufficio Stampa e Propaganda MASERATI
Poligrafica Bodoniana Bologna

Maserati Elettrocarro	section 3-6	
GLI ELETTROMOBILI INDUSTRIALI (REPRINTED)		
black & white brochure with color	11¾ x 8¼"	29.7 x 21 cm	Italian	Style 1

Cover:
Background - black and white illustration
Trucks - red
GLI ELETTROMOBILI INDUSTRIALI - red outlined in black
e la loro dif nel mon - black
Pub a cura della S.A. ALFIERI MASERATI - MODENA - white

Page 2:
Background - white
Heading blocks - blue
Print - black
Heading print 2-7 - white

Maserati Elettrocarro

GLI ELETTROMOBILI INDUSTRIALI (REPRINTED)

black &white brochure with color | 11¾ x 8¼" | 29.7 x 21 cm | Italian | Style 1

section 3-6

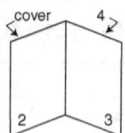

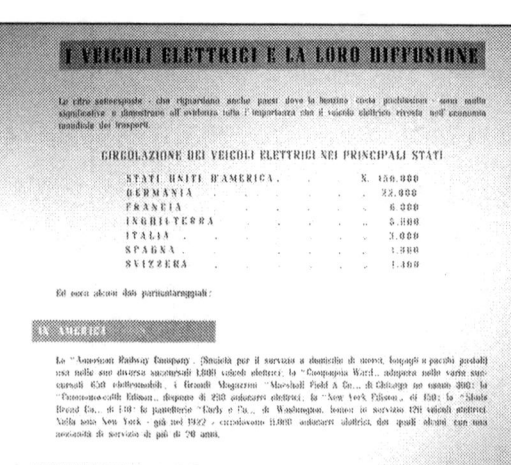

Page 3:
Background - white
Heading blocks - blue
Print - black
Heading blocks print 2-5 - white

Page 4:
Background - white
Bottom border - blue
Maserai emblem - black
ELETTROVEICOLI INDUSTRIALI - blue
Print - black

Marked:
1. E22 - Ufficio Stampa e Propaganda Maserati
Poligrafica Bodoniana Bologna
2. 1998 Archivio Maserati reproduzione anastatica
(Page 4, lower left)

Maserati Elettrocarro	section 3-7

GLI AUTOCARRI ELETTRICI MASERATI (REPRINTED)

| black & white brochure with color cover | 11³/₄ x 8¹/₄" | 30 x 21 cm | Italian | Style 1 |

Cover:
Background - blue top fade to grey bottom
Bottom border - red with white print
Truck - blue
GLI autocarri elettrici - red
MASERATI - red
Print - black

Page 2:
Background:
    left/right border - white
    center - blue
Print - black
ELETTROVEICOLI INDUSTRIALI - red

Maserati Elettrocarro

GLI AUTOCARRI ELETTRICI MASERATI (REPRINTED)

black & white brochure with color cover | 11³/₄ x 8¹/₄" | 30 x 21 cm | Italian | section 3-7 | Style 1

Page 3:
Background:
　　　left/right border - white
　　　center - blue
Print - black
ELETTROVEICOLI INDUSTRIALI - red

Page 4:
Background - white
ELETTROVEICOLI INDUSTRIALI - red
Print - black
Bottom border - blue

Marked:
1. E23 - Ufficio Stampa e Propaganda MASERATI
Poligrafica Bodoniana-Bologna
2. 1998 Archivio Maserati reproduzione anastatica

Maserati Elettrocarro

AUTOCARRO EC 20

black and white brochure with color | 11³/₄ x 8¹/₄" | 30 x 21 cm | Italian | Style 1

Cover:

Page 2:

Maserati Elettrocarro

AUTOCARRO EC 20

black and white brochure with color	11¾ x 8¼"	30 x 21 cm	Italian	Style 1

section 3-8

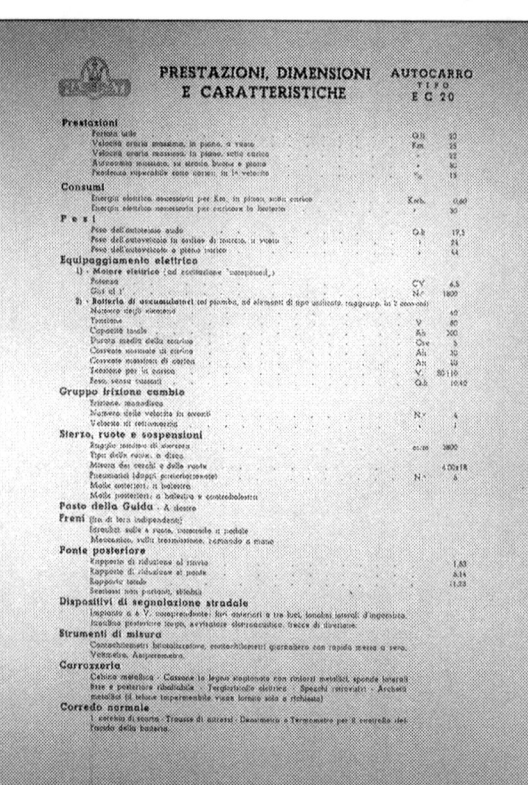

Page 3:
Background -

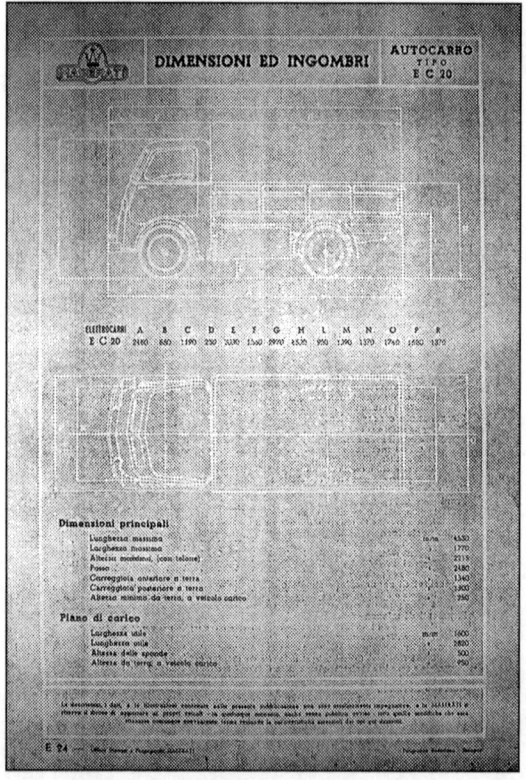

Page 4:
Background -

Marked:
E24 - Ufficio Stampa e Propaganda MASERATI
Poligrafica Bodoniana-Bologna

Maserati Elettrocarro

section 3-9

MASERATI EC.35

| black and white sheet | 11 x 8¾" | 28 x 21.8 cm | Italian | Style 2B |

Front:
Background - white
Maserti badge - blue and red
Print - black
Paper - vellum

Rear:
Blank

Marked:
P.L. CCUDLER-ZABARELLA 2-PADOVA

From the collection of Dr. Adolfo Orsi

36	Maserati Elettrocarro		section 3-10	
	AUTOCARRO EC35			
	color folder	11¾ x 8¼" — 30 x 21 cm	Italian	Style 1

Cover:
Background - dark green
Truck - red
35 - red
Maserati - red
EC - white
Autocarro Elettrico - white

Page 2:
Background - white
Top and bottom band - green
Print - black

Maserati Elettrocarro

AUTOCARRO EC35

| color folder | 11³/₄ x 8¹/₄" | 30 x 21 cm | Italian | Style 1 |

section 3-10

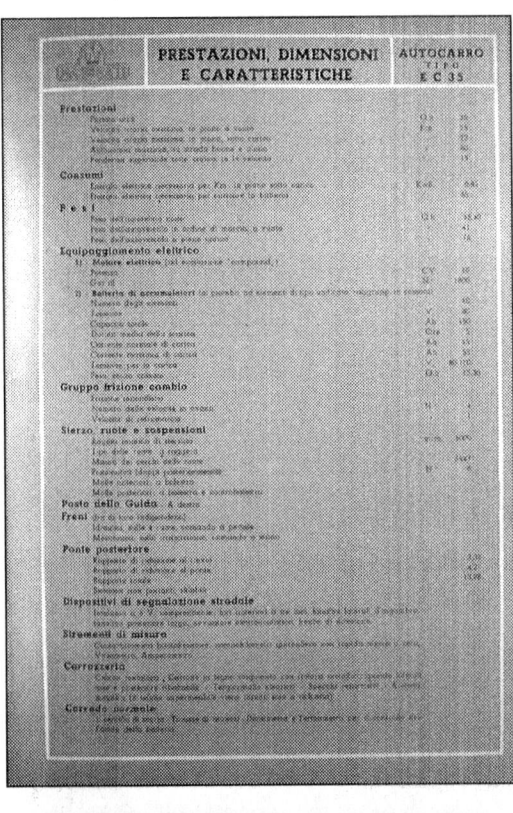

Page 3:
Background - green
Border - white
Print - black

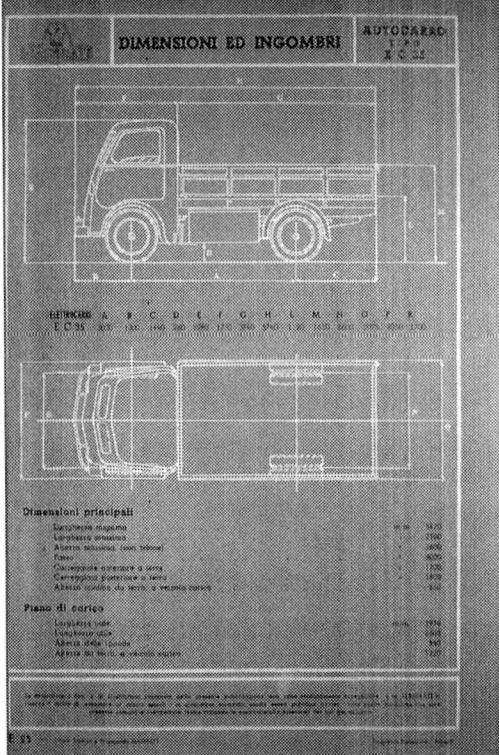

Page 4:
Background - green
Borders, outline of truck and dimension lines - white
Print - black

Marked:
E25 - Ufficio Stampa e Propaganda MASERATI
Poligrafica Bodoniana Bologna

From the collection of Dr. Adolfo Orsi

MOTORI MOTONAUTICA

4.0

MOTORI MOTONAUTICA   4-1

MOTORI MOTONAUTICA PRODUZIONE 1962   4-2

MOTORI MOTONAUTICA

black and white sheet	11³/₄ x 8³/₈"	30 x 21 cm	Italian	Style 2B

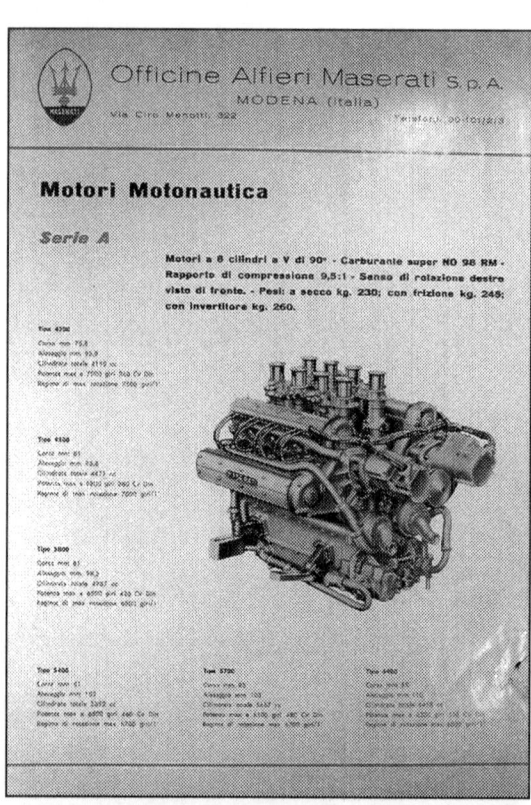

Front:
Background - white
Maserati badge - blue and red
Horizontal stripes - red
Serie A - red
Print - black
Motor - black and white photo

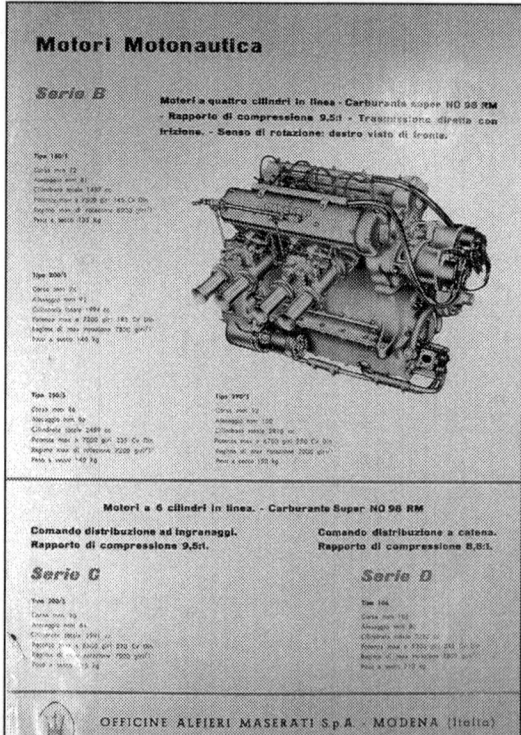

Rear:
Background - white
MASERATI badge - blue and red
Series B,C,D - red
Print - black

Marked:
None

MOTORI MOTONAUTICA PRODUZIONE 1962

| Motori Motonautica | section 4-2 | 41 |
| black and white sheet | 11¹¹/₁₆ x 8¹/₄" | 29.7 x 21 cm | Italian | Style 2B |

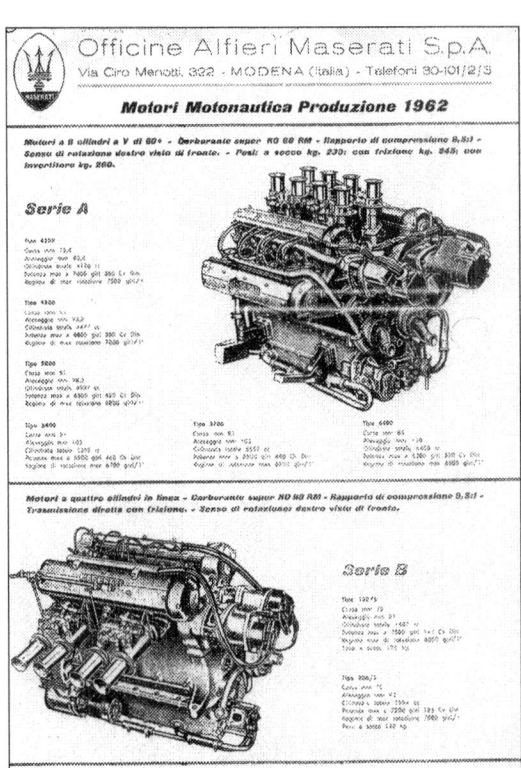

Front:
Background - white
Maserati badge - blue and red
Horizontal stripes - red
Series A, B - red
Print - black
Motor - black and white photos

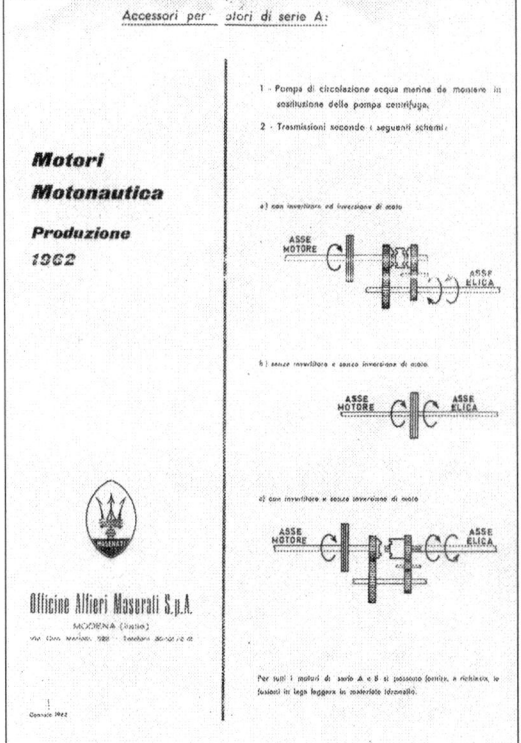

Rear:
Background - white
MASERATI badge - blue and red
Print - black

Marked:
Gennaio 1962

From the collection of Dr. Adolfo Orsi

Maserati Post War Brochures through Inline 6 Cylinder Cars

A6 SERIES

5.0

A6 1500 cm^3 - MARS 1947/8 (OVERPRINTED 1948)	5-1
A6 - GIUGNO 1947	5-2
A6 1500 cc - 1947	5-3
A6 1500 cc - 1947	5-4
A6GCS 2000 cc - MARZO 1948	5-5
A6G 4 1948	5-6
TIPO A6GCS 2000 cc - SETTEMBRE 1948 *	5-7
A6 1500 cc - 1949 (REPRINTED)	5-8
A6G 2000 cm^3 - 1951	5-9
A6G 2000 cm^3 - 1951	5-10
TIPO A6GCS/2000 CC - 7 - 1951 *	5-11
A6GCM/2000 MONOPOSTO F2 - 7 - 1951 *	5-12
TIPO A6GCS/2000 CC *	5-13
A6G/2000 1955	5-14
SPORT 2000 - 1954 (REPRINTED)	5-15
"2000" GRAN TURISMO - 1956 (REPRINTED)	5-16
GRAN TURISMO A6G 2000/A 1957	5-17
GRAN TURISMO A6G 2000/B 1957	5-18
GRAN TURISMO A6G 2000/C 1957	5-19
GRAN TURISMO A6G 2000/D 1957	5-20

* NOTE: Many different "blue line" specification pages were issued as needed.

44	**A6 Series**		section 5-1	cover 4 / 2 3
	A6 1500 cm³ - MARS 1947/8 (OVERPRINTED 1948)			
	black and white folder	9⁵/₈ x 7¹/₄" 24.4 x 18.5 cm	French	Style 1

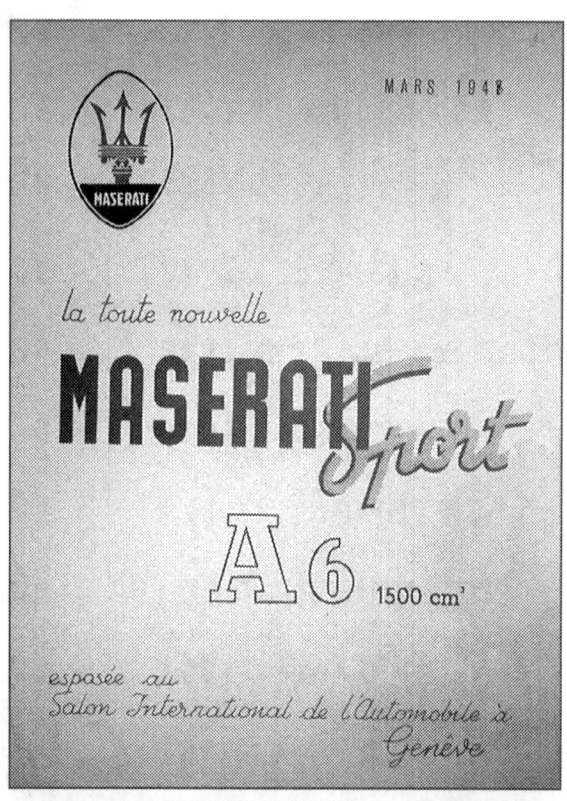

Cover:
Background - off white
Maserati badge - blue and red
A6 1500 cm³ - red
Print - grey

1947 version had vellum page in Italian glued inside listing. Technical specifications as per section 5-3, page 3

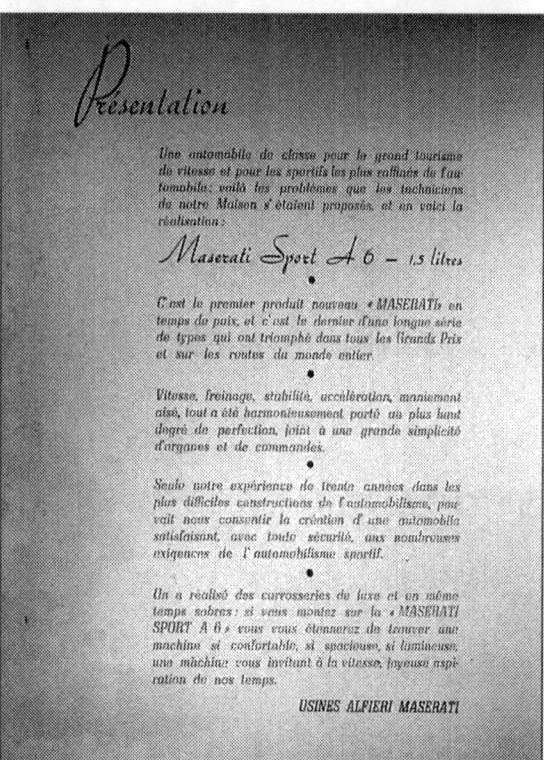

Page 2:
Background - off white
P - blue
Maserati Sport A6 - 1.5 litres - blue
Usines Alfieri Maserati - blue
Print - grey

A6 Series			section 5-1		45
A6 1500 cm³ - MARS 1947/8 (OVERMARKED 1948)					
black and white folder	9⅝ x 7¼"	24.4 x 18.5 cm	French	Style 1	

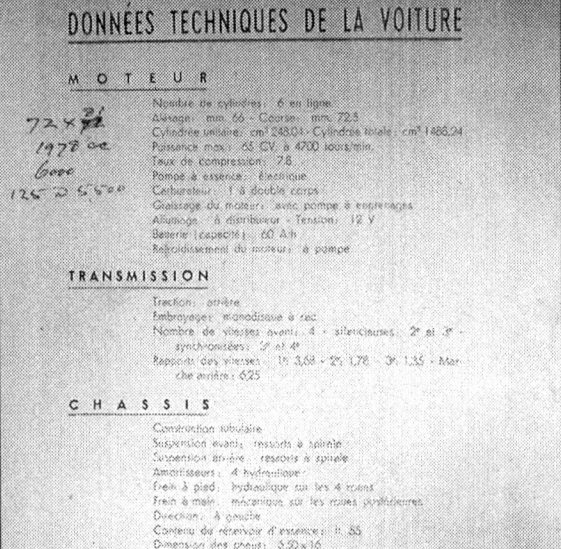

Page 3:
Background - off white
Headings - blue
Print - grey

Page 4:
Background - off white
Maserati badge - blue and red
Print - grey

Marked:
1. First issued 1947
2. Overprinted in blue with 8 for 1948

Artigrafiche Modenesi - Modena

A6 Series

A6 - GIUGNO 1947

| black and white sheet | 11³/₄ x 8¹/₄" | 30 x 21 cm | Italian | Style 2B |

Front:
Background - white
Print - black

Rear:
Background - white
Blank

Marked:
Mod 87 500 9-47

A6 Series			section 5-3	cover	47
A6 1500 cc - 1947					
grey and white folder	9³/₈ x 7"	24 x 18 cm	Italian	Style 1	

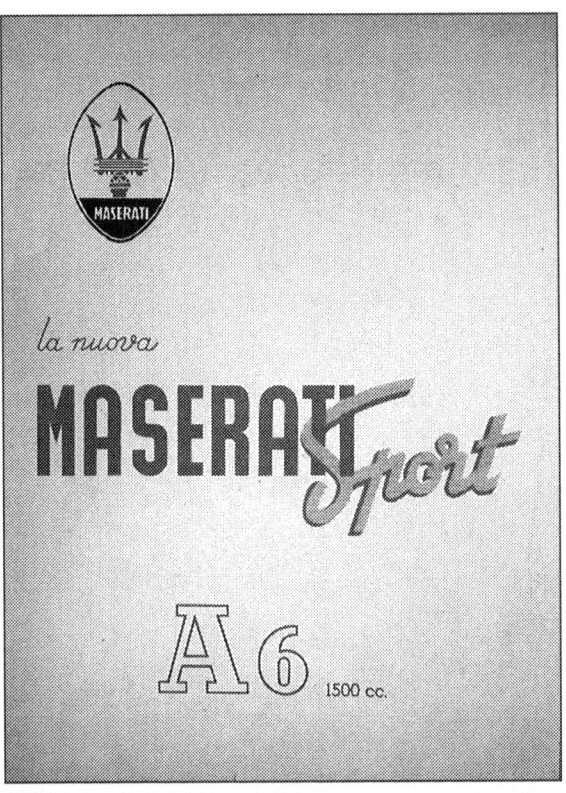

Cover:
Background - off white
Maserati badge - blue and red
A6 1500cc - red
Print - grey

Page 2:
Background - off white
P - blue
Maserati Sport A6 - 1500cc - blue
Officine Alfieri Maserati - blue
Print - grey

48	**A6 Series**	section 5-3	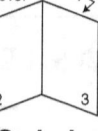
	A6 1500 cc - 1947		
	grey and white folder	9³/₈ x 7" 24 x 18 cm Italian	Style 1

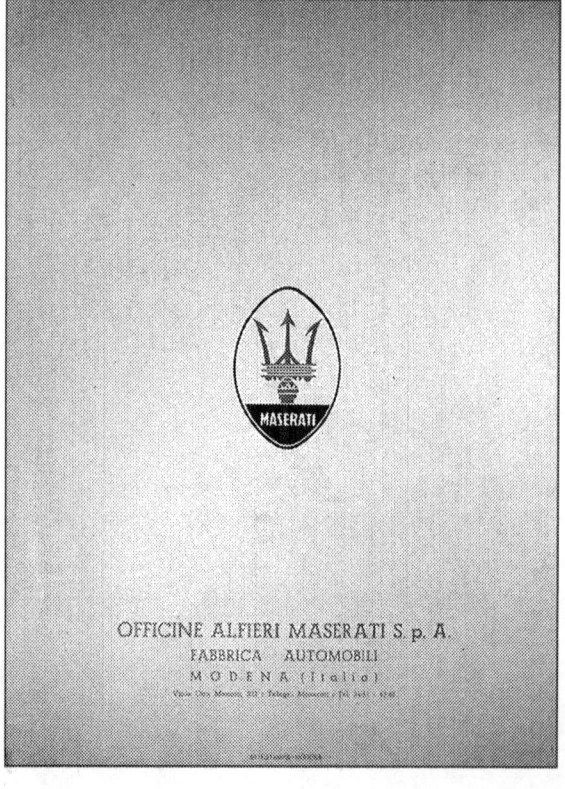

Page 3:
Background - off white
Heading - blue
Print - grey

Page 4:
Background - off white
Maserati badge - blue and red
Print - grey

Marked:
Artestampa - Modena

A6 Series			section 5-4		49
A6 1500 cc - 1947					
grey and white sheet	9¼ x 6⅞"	23.5 x 17.5 cm	Italian	Style 2B	

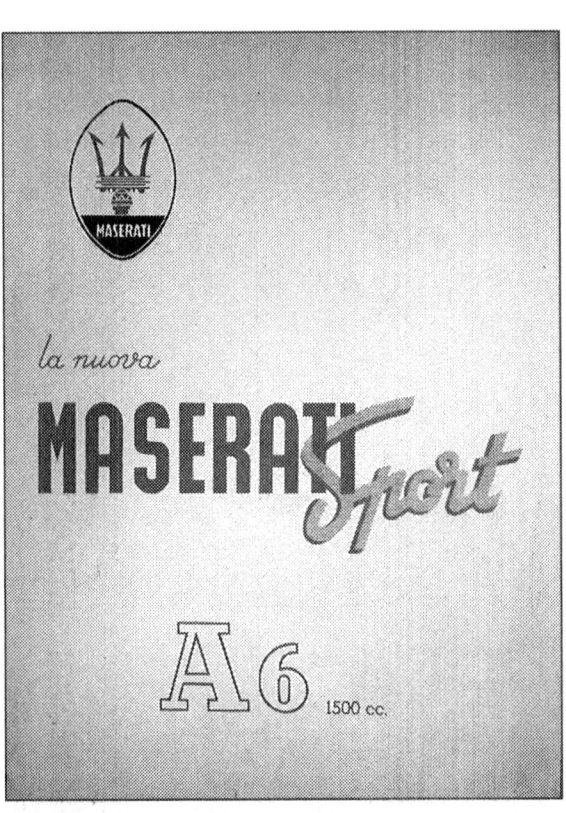

Front:
Background - off white
Maserati badge - blue and red
A6 1500 cc - red
Print - grey

Rear:
Background - off white
Headings - blue
Print - grey

Marked:
None

A6 Series

A6GCS 2000 cc - MARZO 1948

| booklet | ? " | ? cm | Italian | Style 5 |

section 5-5

Cover:
Background - white
Print - black

Marked:
None

Page 2:
Blank

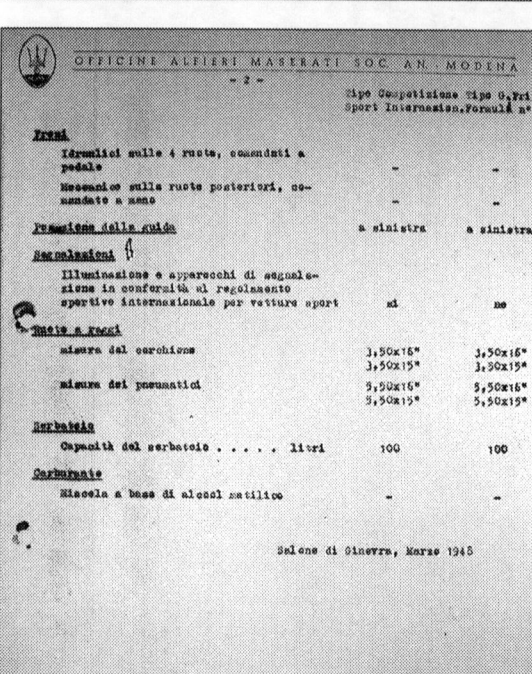

Page 3:
Background - white
Print - ?

Marked:
Mod 123 1500 2-48

Page 4:
Blank

A6 Series			section 5-5	

A6GCS 2000 cc - MARZO 1948

booklet	? "	? cm	Italian	Style 5

Page 5:
Background - white
Photos - black and white

Marked:
Mod 220 1600 7-47

Page 6:
Blank

Page 7:
Background - white
Photos - black and white

Marked:
Mod 220 1600 7-47

Page 8:
Blank

52	A6 Series	section 5-6	
	A6G 4 1948		
	black and white sheet	11³/₄ x 7³/₄" 29.8 x 19.7 cm Italian	Style 2B

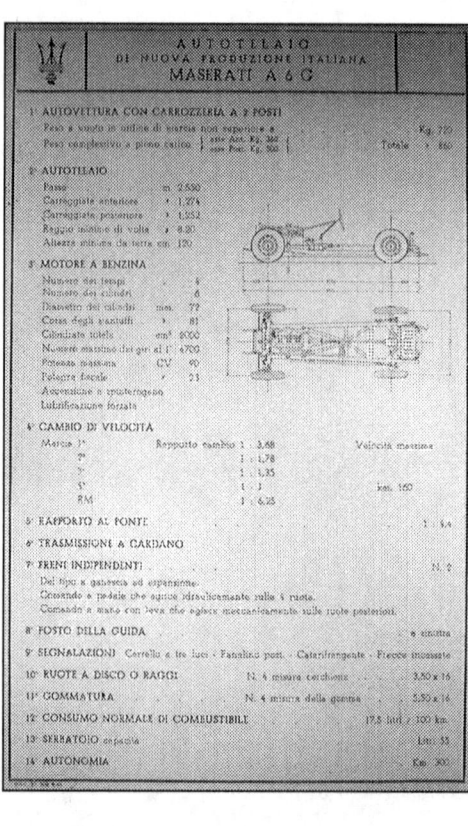

Front:
Background - white
Print - black

Marked:
Mod 87 500 4-48

Rear:
Blank

A6 Series

section 5-7

TIPO A6GCS 2000 cc - SETTEMBRE 1948

| blue line sheet | 11½ x 8¼" | 29.2 x 21 cm | Italian | Style 2B |

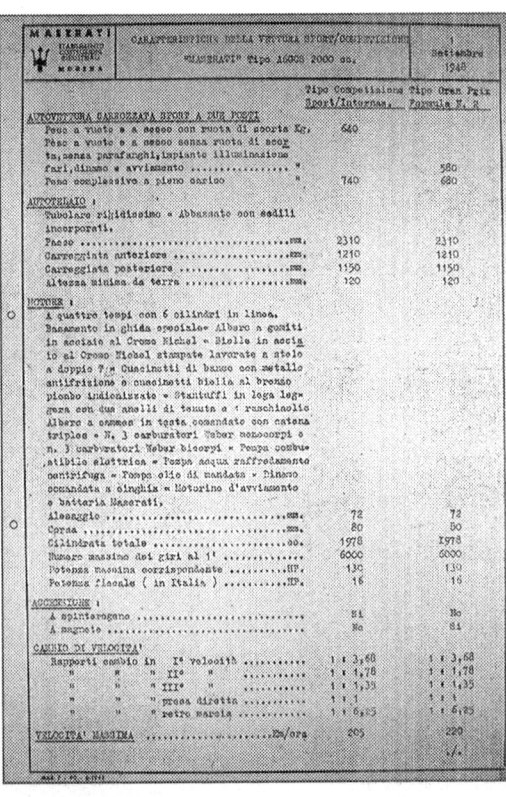

Front:
(Sheet 1)
Background - white
Print - blue

Marked:
Mod 7-90-6-1948

Rear:
Blank

Front:
(Sheet 2)
Background - white
Print - blue

Marked:
Mod 7-90-6-1948

Rear:
Blank

54	**A6 Series**	section 5-8	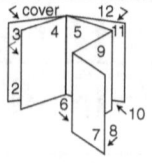
	A6 1500 cc - 1949 (REPRINTED)		
	color brochure — 10½ x 7½" — 26.7 x 19.2 cm — Italian		Style 12

Cover:
Background - blue fading to white around car
Maserati badge - blue and red
Car - dark red

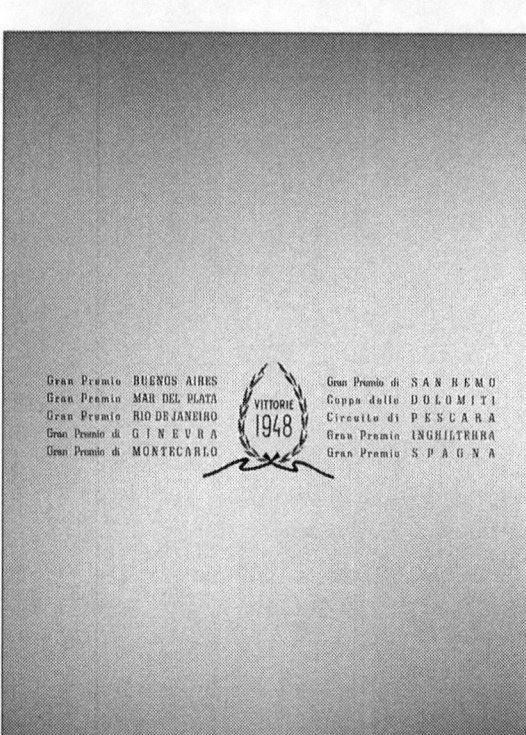

Page 2:
Background - white
Wreath - gold
1948 & Ribbon - blue
Print - black

A6 Series

A6 1500 cc - 1949 (REPRINTED)

| color brochure | 10½ x 7½" | 26.7 x 19.2 cm | Italian | Style 12 |

section 5-8

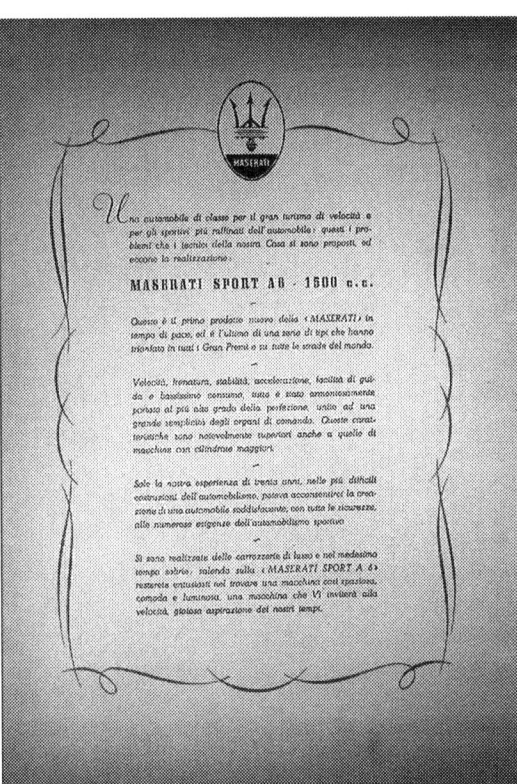

Page 3:
Background - white
Maserati badge - blue and red
Pin stripe - gold
Print - black

Page 4:
Background - white
Car - blue
nel gra - blue
Print - black
Suspension - black and white ilustrations
Specification page - light blue

A6 Series		section 5-8		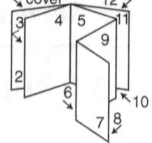
A6 1500 cc - 1949 (REPRINTED)				
color brochure	10½ x 7½" 26.7 x 19.2 cm		Italian	Style 12

Page 5:
Background - white
Motors - black and white illustrations
nel gran turismo - blue
Print - black
Car - yellow with colored illustration

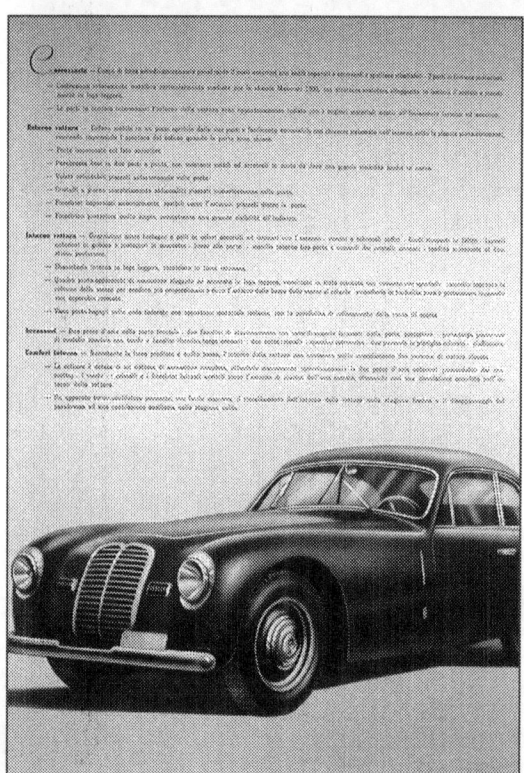

Page 6:
Background - white
Print - black
Car - black and white illustration surrounded with yellow

A6 Series

A6 1500 cc - 1949 (REPRINTED)

| color brochure | 10½ x 7½" | 26.7 x 19.2 cm | Italian | Style 12 |

section 5-8

Page 7:
Background - white shaded to grey around photos
Photos - black and white illustrations

Page 8:
Background -
Top - orange fading to white center with red line connecting black dots, green car with yellow shirt and helmet
Bottom - yellow with black and white cars, white page with black print
Maserati A6 GCS etc - grey

58	**A6 Series**	section 5-8	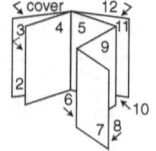
	A6 1500 cc - 1949 (REPRINTED)		
	color brochure	10½ x 7½" 26.7 x 19.2 cm Italian	Style 12

Page 9:
Background - yellow
Print - black
Pictures - black and white illustrations

Page 10:
Background - white
negli auto - blue
Cars - red with blue following with yellow and grey illustration
Print - grey
Motor - black and white illustration

A6 Series

A6 1500 cc - 1949 (REPRINTED)

| color brochure | 10½ x 7½" | 26.7 x 19.2 cm | Italian | Style 12 |

section 5-8

Page 11:
Background -   left - blue
                right - white
Print - black
Car and wheel - black and white illustration

Page 12:
Background - white
Maserati badge - blue and red
Battery - black and white illustration
Spark Plug - black and white illustration
Print - black
Bottom border - grey
Area around illustrations - grey

Marked:
1. OFFICINE GRAFICHE G. VACCARI-SESTO S. G. - MILANO
2. Reprinted - Same size - 1998 Archivo Maserati reproduzione anastatica
(Page 12, lower left)

60	**A6 Series**	section 5-9	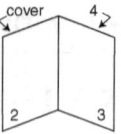
	A6G 2000 cm³ - 1951		
	black and white folder	9¼ x 6⅞"	23.5 x 17.6 cm	Italian	Style 1

Cover:
Background - off white
Maserati badge - blue and red print - grey
A6G 2000 cm³ - red

Page 2:
Background - off white
P - blue
Maserati Sport A6G 2 litri - blue
OFFICINE ALFIERI MASERATI - blue
Print - grey

A6 Series

A6G 2000 cm³ - 1951

| black and white folder | 9¼ x 6⅞" | 23.5 x 17.6 cm | Italian | Style 1 |

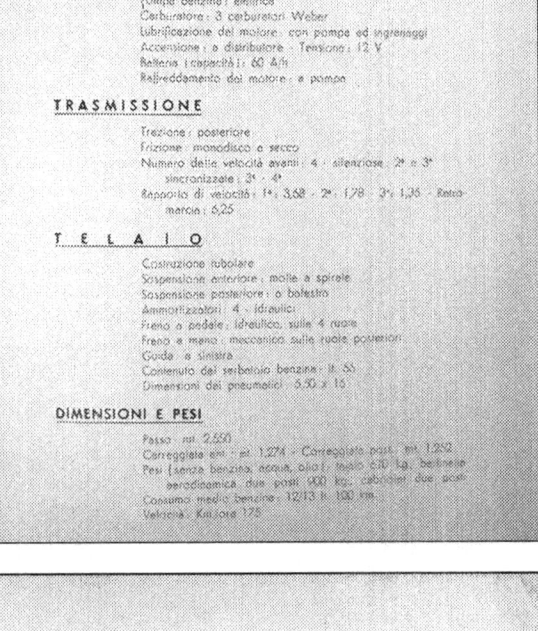

Page 3:
Background - off white
Headings - blue
Print and underline - grey

Page 4:
Background - off white
Maserati badge - blue and red
Print - grey
Spark plug - grey
Battery - grey

Marked:
ARTI GRAFICHE MODENESI - 1951

62	**A6 Series**	section 5-10	cover 4 / 2 3
	A6 G 2000 cm³ - 1951		
	black and white folder	9⁵/₈ x 6⁷/₈" 24.6 x 17.6 cm	French	Style 1

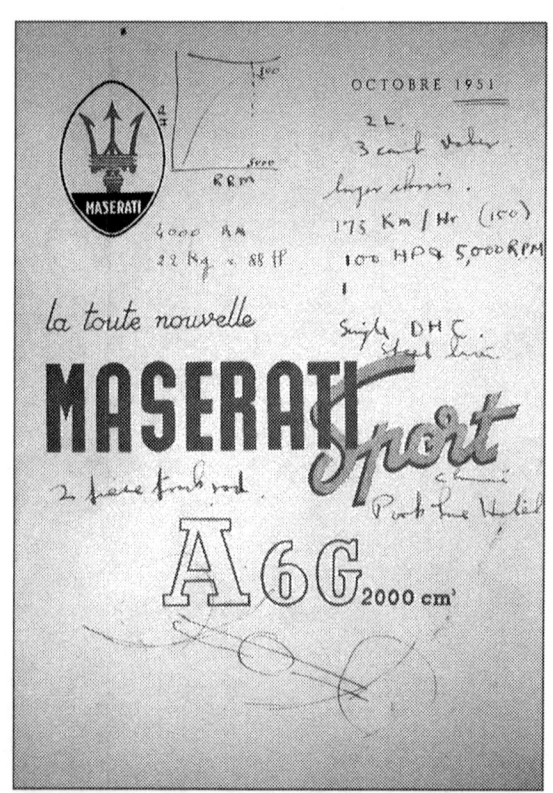

Cover:
Background - off white
Maserati badge - blue and red
A6G 2000 cm^3 - red
Print - grey

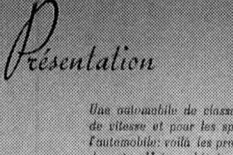

Page 2:
Background - off white
P - blue
Maserati Sport A6G 2 litres - blue
USINES ALFIERI MASERATI - blue
Dots - blue
Print - grey

A6 Series		section 5-10		63
A6 G 2000 cm³ - 1951				
black and white folder	9⁵/₈ x 6⁷/₈" 24.6 x 17.6 cm	French		Style 1

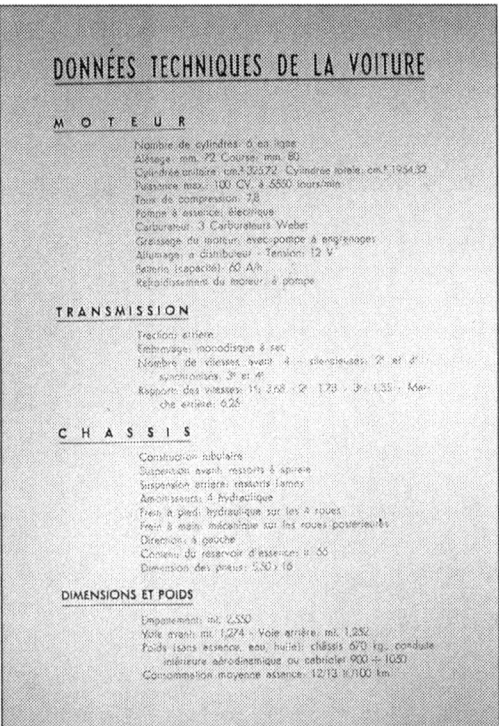

Page 3:
Background - off white
Heading - blue
Print - grey

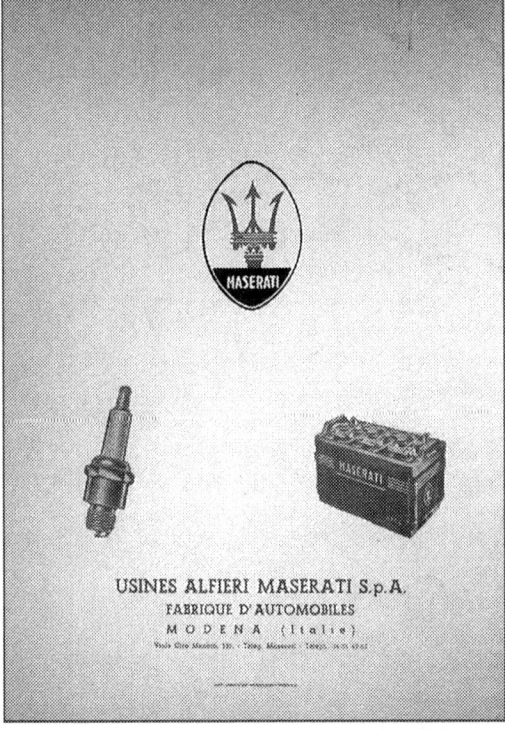

Page 4:
Background - off white
Maserati badge - blue and red
Print - grey
Spark plug - grey
Battery - grey

Marked:
ARTI GRAFICHE MODENESI - MODENA

A6 Series

section 5-11

TIPO A6GCS/2000 cc - 7 - 1951

| blue line sheet | 11½ x 8¼" | 29.2 x 21 cm | Italian | Style 2B |

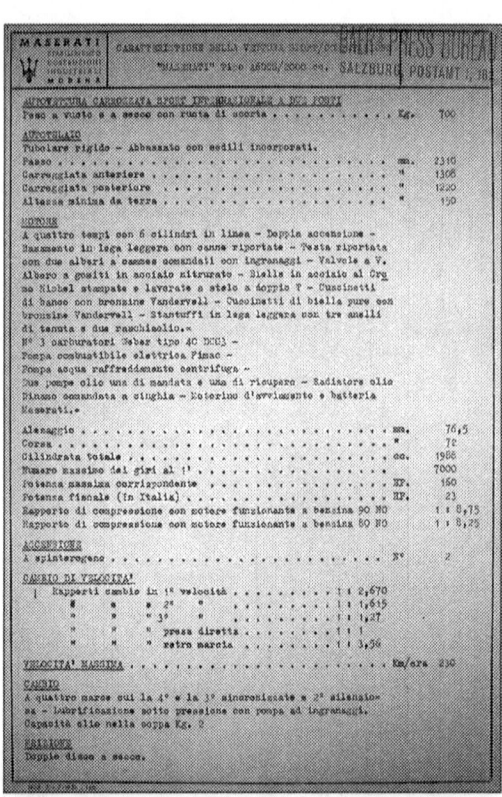

Front:
(Sheet 1)
Background - white
Print - blue

Marked:
Mod. 7-7-1951-180

Rear:
Background - white
Blank

Front:
(Sheet 2)
Background - white
Print - blue

Marked:
Mod. 7-7-1951-180

Rear:
Background - white
Blank

A6 Series

A6GCM/2000 MONOPOSTO F2 - 7 - 1951

section 5-12

65

| blue line sheet | 11 1/2 x 8 3/4" | 29.2 x 21 cm | Italian | Style 2B |

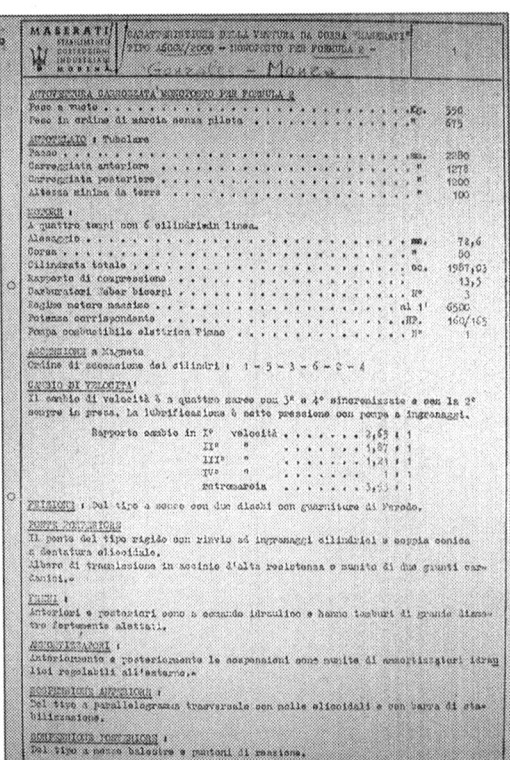

Front:
(Sheet 1)
Background - white
Print - blue

Marked:
Mod 7 - 7 - 1951 - 180

Rear:
Background - white
Blank

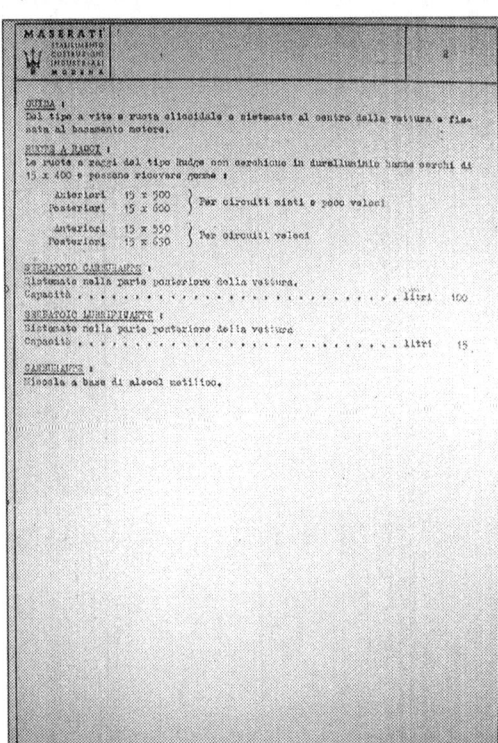

Front:
(Sheet 2)
Background - white
Print - blue

Marked:
Mod 7 - 7 - 1951 - 180

Rear:
Background - white
Blank

A6 Series

TIPO A6GCS/2000 cc

section 5-13

| blue line sheet | 11½ x 8¼" | 29.2 x 21 cm | Italian | Style 2B |

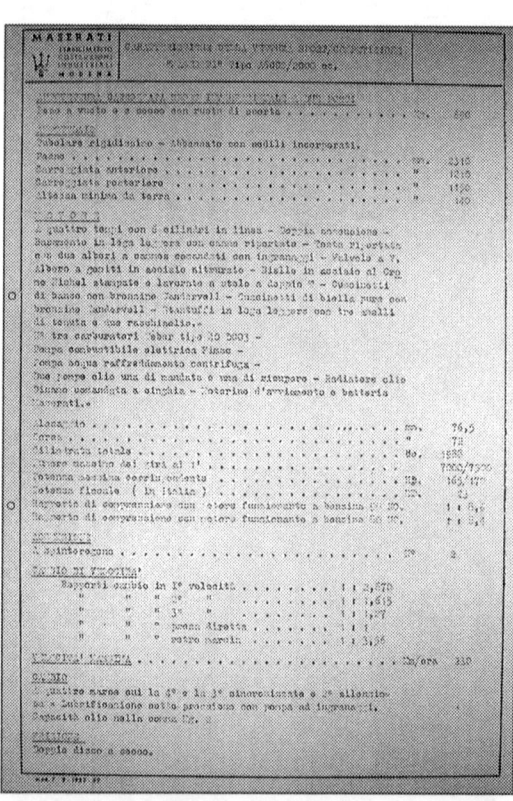

Front:
(Sheet 1)
Background - white
Print - blue

Marked:
Mod. 7 9 - 1952 - 99

Rear:
Background - white
Blank

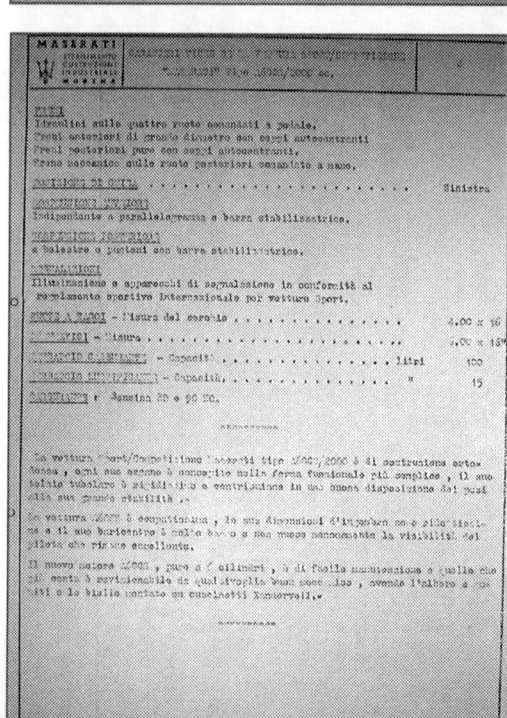

Front:
(Sheet 2)
Background - white
Print - blue

Marked:
Mod. 7 9 - 1952 - 99

Rear:
Background - white
Blank

A6 Series			section 5-14	
A6G/2000 1955				67
blue and white folder	8⁵/₈ x 6¹/₄"	22 x 16 cm	Italian	Style 1

Cover:
Background - white
Maserati badge - blue and red
Maserati - red
Print - dark blue

This photograph was normally included with this brochure. Today they are rarely found together.

Page 2:
Background - white
Print - dark blue

68	**A6 Series**	section 5-14	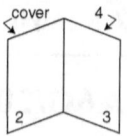	
	A6G/2000			
	blue and white folder	8⅝ x 6¼"	22 x 16 cm	Italian	Style 1

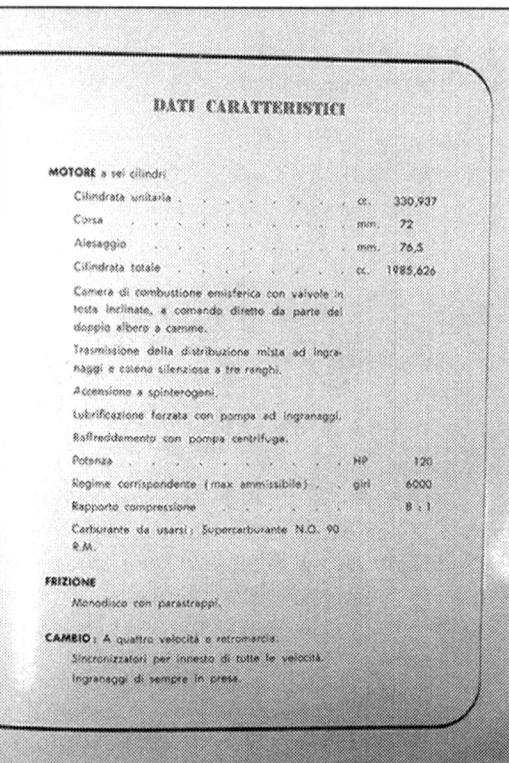

Page 3:
Background - white
Print - dark blue
Heading - red

Page 4:
Background - white
Print - dark blue

Marked:
None

A6 Series

SPORT 2000 - 1954 (REPRINTED)

1,3 color brochure orig / reprint	8¼ x 11¼"	21 x 28.5 cm	Italian	Style 13
2 color brochure reprint	8³/₈ x 11⅛"	21.3 x 28.3 cm		

section 5-15

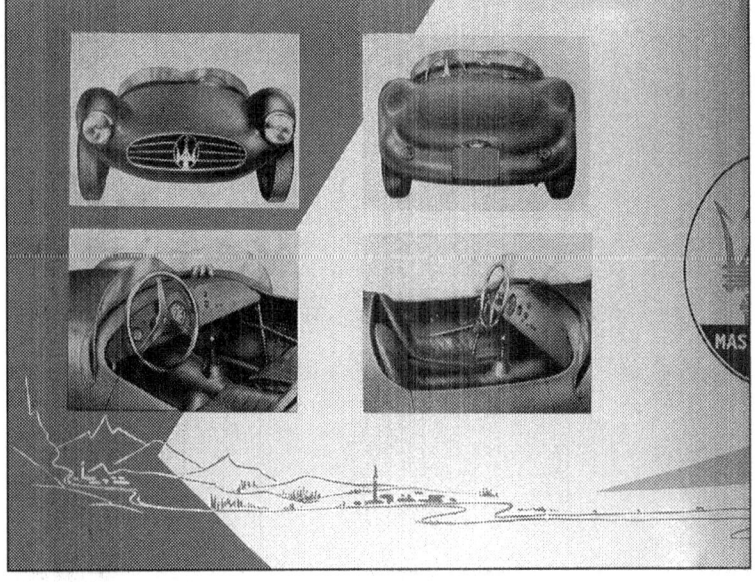

Cover:
Background - white
Maserati badge - blue and red
Maserati - red
Car - red
Flag - black and white
Shaded background - grey to white

Page 2:
Background: left - red
              right - white
Maserati badge - blue and red
Illustrations - black and white

A6 Series

SPORT 2000 - 1954 (REPRINTED)

section 5-15

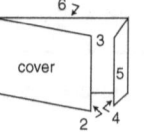

Style 13

1,3 color brochure orig / reprint	8¼ x 11¼"	21 x 28.5 cm	Italian	
2 color brochure reprint	8³⁄₈ x 11⅛"	21.3 x 28.3 cm		

Page 3:
Background - grey
Bottom border - white
Graphics - red
Illustrations - black and white on light grey background
Maserati badge - blue and red

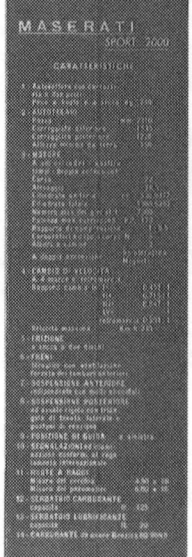

Page 4:
Background - red
Print - white

A6 Series

SPORT 2000 - 1954 (REPRINTED)

1, 3 color brochure orig / reprint	8¼ x 11¼"	21 x 28.5 cm	Italian	Style 13
2 color brochure reprint	8⅜ x 11⅛"	21.3 x 28.3 cm		

section 5-15

Page 5
Background - black
Illustrations - white

Page 6
Background - white
Maserati badge - blue and red
Top band - red with white print
Bottom border - grey with red print
Print - black

Marked
1. Stab. Pol. Artioli - Modena 8¼ x 11¼"
2. 1998 Archivio Maserati riproduzione anastatica 8⅜ x 11⅛"
(Page 6, lower right)
3. RPI 2020 7-89 (Australia) 8¼ x 11¼"

A6 Series

"2000" GRAN TURISMO - 1956 (REPRINTED)

| 1, 2 b&w brochure orig | 8¼ x 11¾" | 21 x 29.8 cm | ITA, FRA, ENG | Style 3 |
| 3 b&w brochure reprint | 8 x 11¹¹⁄₁₆" | 20.4 x 30 cm | | |

section 5-16

Cover:
Background - blue
Maserati badge - blue and red
Stripe - white
Print - black

Page 2:
Background - white
Triangle around motor - yellow
Print - black
Motor - black and white illustartion

A6 Series

section 5-16 | 73

"2000" GRAN TURISMO - 1956 (REPRINTED)

| 1, 2 b&w brochure orig | 8¼ x 11¾" | 21 x 29.8 cm | ITA, FRA, ENG | Style 3 |
| 3 b&w brochure reprint | 8 x 11¹¹⁄₁₆" | 20.4 x 30 cm | | |

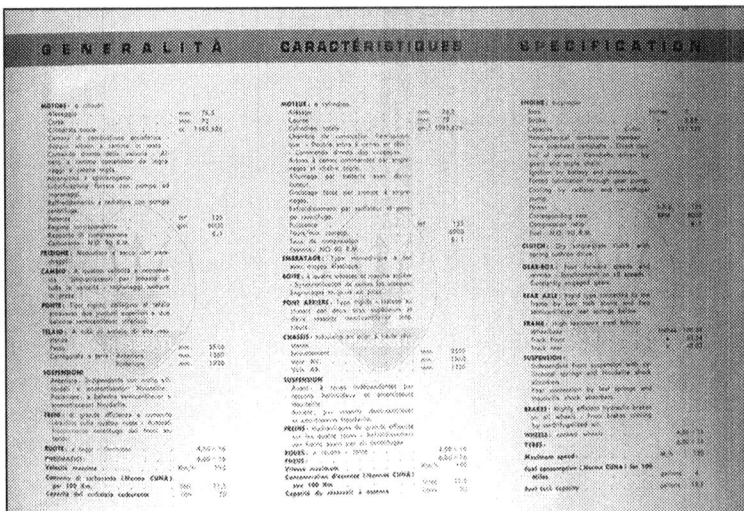

Page 3:
Background - white
Top band - blue
Print - black
Maserati badge - yellow

Page 4:
Photograph - black and white /A
Band - white
Print - blue

74	**A6 Series**	section 5-16	
	"2000" GRAN TURISMO - 1956 (REPRINTED)		
	1, 2 b&w brochure orig 8¼ x 11¾" 21 x 29.8 cm	ITA, FRA, ENG	Style 3
	3 b&w brochure reprint 8 x 11¹¹⁄₁₆" 20.4 x 30 cm		

Page 5:
Photograph - black and white / B
Band - blue
Print - black

Page 6:
Photograph - black and white / C
Band - blue
Print - black

A6 Series			section 5-16	

"2000" GRAN TURISMO - 1956 (REPRINTED)

1, 2 b&w brochure orig	8¼ x 11¾"	21 x 29.8 cm	ITA, FRA, ENG	Style 3
3 b&w brochure reprint	8 x 11¹¹⁄₁₆"	20.4 x 30 cm		

Page 7:
Photograph - black and white / D
Band - white
Print - blue

Page 8:
Background - white
Stripes - blue
Print - black

Marked:
1. Stab. Pol. Artioli - Modena 8¼ x 11¾"
2. 2000 - 2 - 58 - Stab. Pol. Artioli - Modena 8¼ x 11¾"
3. 1998 Archivio Maserati Ripoduzione Anastatica 2000 - 2 - 58 - Stab. Pol. Artioli - Modena 8 x 11¹¹⁄₁₆" (Page 8, lower left)
4. RPI 2018-1988 (Australia) 8¼ x 11¼"

A6 Series	section 5-17	
GRAN TURISMO A6G 2000/A 1957		
color sheet	8 x 11⁵⁄₈"	21.4 x 29.5 cm	ITA, FRA, ENG	Style 2A

Front:
Background - light green
Maserati badge - blue and red
Car - black and white illustration
Stripe - white
Print - black

Rear:
Background - white
Headings - red
OFFICINE ALFIERI MASERATI
S.p.A. - red
Maserati badge - light green
Print - black

Marked:
Stab. Pol. Artioli - Modena

A6 Series				section 5-18		77
GRAN TURISMO A6G 2000/B 1957						
color sheet	8 x 11 5/8"	20.4 x 29.5 cm	ITA, FRA, ENG		Style 2A	

Brochure exists; however, a copy was not available for this book.

A6 Series

GRAN TURISMO A6G 2000/C 1957

section 5-19

| color sheet | 8 x 11⁵⁄₈" | 21.4 x 29.5 cm | ITA, FRA, ENG | Style 2A |

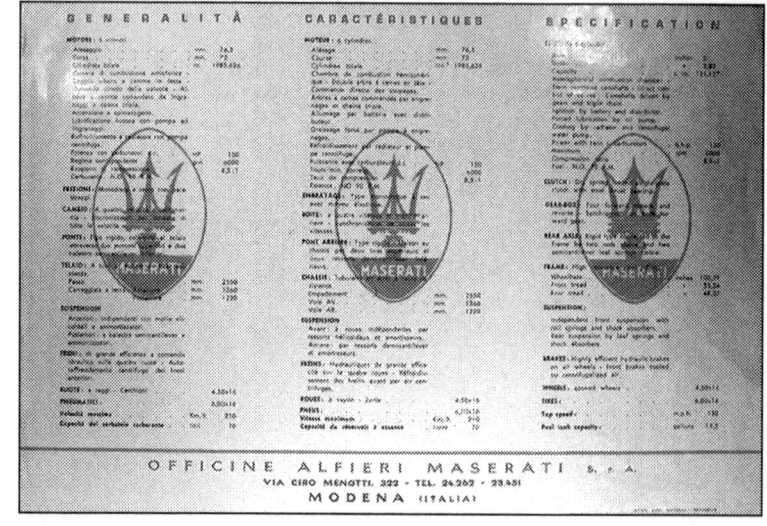

Front:
Background - light blue
Maserati badge - blue and red
Car - black and white illustration
Stripe - white
Print - black

Rear:
Background - white
Headings - red
Officine Alfieri Maserati S.p.A - ?
Maserati badge - blue and red
Print - black

Marked:
Stab. Pol. Artioli - Modena

A6 Series	section 5-20	
GRAN TURISMO A6G 2000/D 1957		79
color sheet	8 x 11⁵⁄₈"	21.4 x 29.5 cm	ITA, FRA, ENG	Style 2A

Front:
Background - light yellow
Maserati badge - blue and red
Car - black and white illustration
Stripe - white
Print - black

Rear:
Background - white
Headings - red
Officine Alfieri Maserati S.p.A
Print - black

Marked:
Stab. Pol. Artioli - Modena

COMPETITION CARS

6.0

4CLT/48 1500cc SETTEMBRE 1948*	6-1
SPORT 150/S (REPRINTED)	6-2
SPORT 150/S (REPRINTED)	6-3
TIPO 150/S - 1500 CC	6-4
TIPO 200/S 2000 cc - 2-56	6-5
TIPO 200/SI 2000 cc - 9-56	6-6
SPORT 200 SI	6-7
SPORT 200 SI - 3-57, 10-57 (REPRINTED)	6-8
TIPO 250/S - 6-54*	6-9
TIPO 250/F - FORMULA 1*	6-10
LA NUOVA VETTURA MASERATI SPORT 3000 cc	6-11
TIPO 300/S - 6-54*	6-12
TIPO 300/S - 3-55*	6-13
TIPO 300/S - 3000cc - 2-56	6-14
SPORT 300S (REPRINTED)	6-15
SPORT 300S - 6-57, 10-57	6-16
SPORT 450/S	6-17
SPORT 450/S - 6-57, 10-57 (REPRINTED)	6-18

COMPETITION CARS

6.0

CARATTERISTICHE DELLE NUOVA VETTURE SPORT 6-19
MASERATI - 4 CILINDRI TIPO 60, TIPO 61

VETTURETTA MASERATI TIPO SPORT 6-20

*NOTE: MANY DIFFERENT ONE SIDED "BLUE LINE" PAGES ISSUED AS NEEDED.

Competition Cars			section 6-1		

4CLT/48 1500cc SETTEMBRE 1948*

blue line sheet	11 x 8⁹/₁₆"	28 x 21.8 cm	Italian	Style 2A

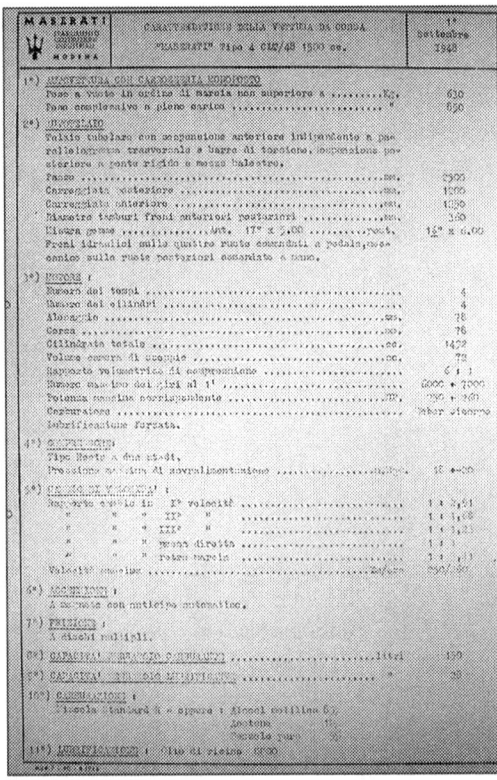

Front:
Background - white
Print - blue

Marked
Mod. 7-90-6-1948

Rear:
Background - white
Blank

*NOTE: MANY DIFFERENT ONE SIDED "BLUE LINE" PAGES ISSUED AS NEEDED.

Competition Cars	section 6-2	
84 **SPORT 150/S (REPRINTED)**		
1, 2 colored folder original 3 colored folder reprint	8 x 11¾" 8⅛ x 11¹³⁄₁₆"	20.5 x 30 cm 20.7 x 30.1 cm	ITA, FRA, ENG	Style 1

Cover:
Background - medium blue
Maserati badge - blue and red
Band - red with black print

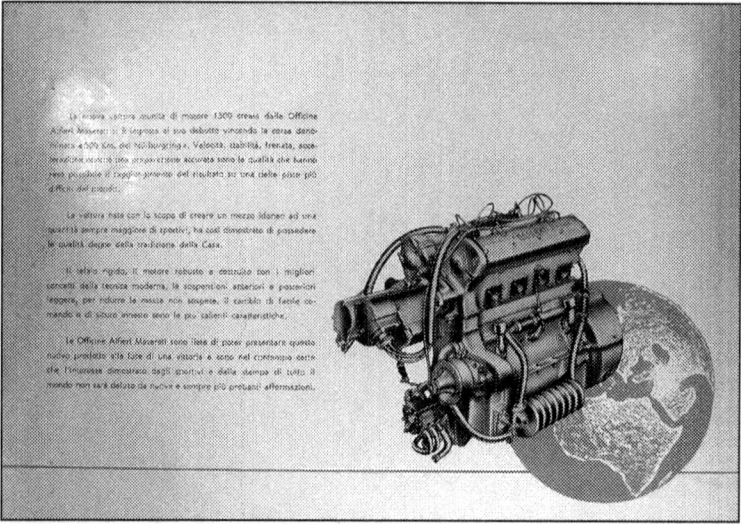

Page 2:
Background - white
Engine - black and white photo
Print - black
Stripe - red
World - blue

Competition Cars		section 6-2	cover 4 / 2 3	
SPORT 150/S (REPRINTED)				85
1, 2 colored folder original 3 colored folder reprint	8 x 11¾" 8⅛ x 11¹³⁄₁₆"	20.5 x 30 cm 20.7 x 30.1 cm	ITA, FRA, ENG	Style 1

Page 3:
Background - white
Left band - blue
Car - red
Picture - black and white photo
Print - black

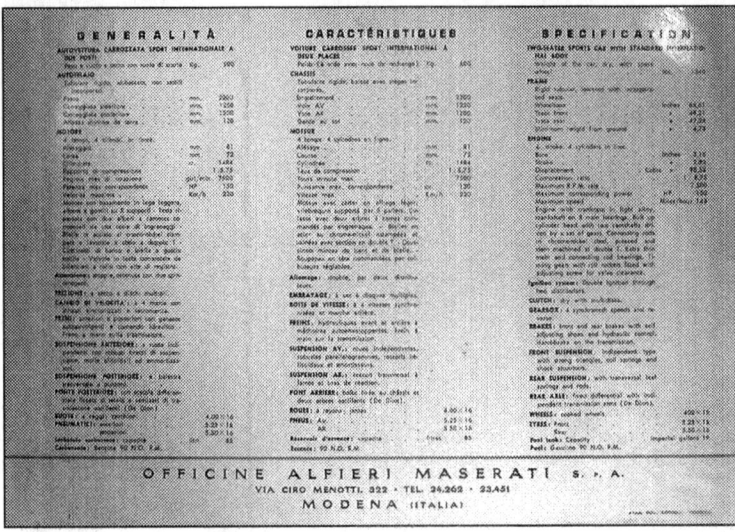

Page 4:
Background - white
Print - black
Stripe - blue

Marked
1,2. Stab. Pol. Artioli - Modena
3. RPI 2016 - 1988 (Australia)

Competition Cars	section 6-3	
SPORT 150/S		

colored sheet original	8³/₁₆ x 11⁷/₈"	21 x 30.3 cm	Italian	Style 2A
colored sheet reprint	8¹/₈ x 11¹¹/₁₆"	20.7 x 29.7 cm		

86

Front:
Background - blue
Maserati badge - blue, red and white background
Car - black and white photo
Band - red with black print

Rear:
Background - white
Print - black
Engine - black and white photo
Stripe - red
Wold - blue

Marked:
1. Blank
2. Stab. Pol. Artioli - Modena
3. 1998 Archivio Maserati
riproduzione anastatica (Lower left corner)

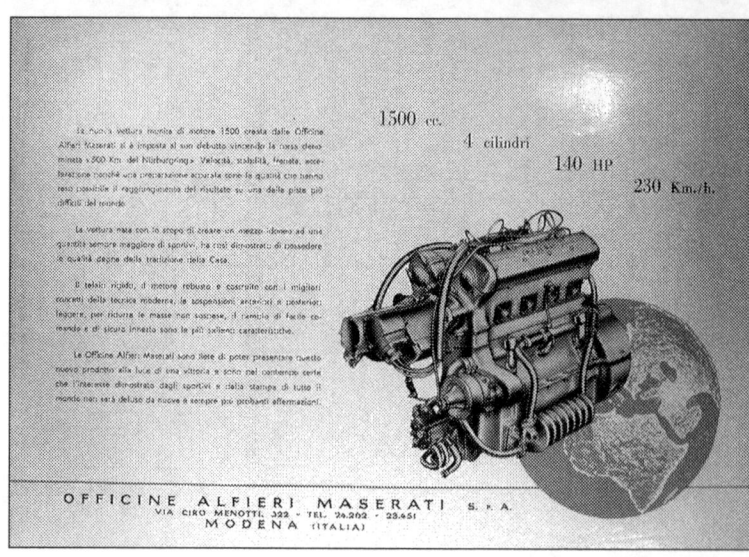

Competition Cars	section 6-4
TIPO 150/S - 1500 cc	

| blue and white folder | 8⅝ x 6¼" | 22 x 16 cm | Italian | Style 1 |

Cover:
Background - white
Maserati badge - blue and red
Maserati - red
Print - dark blue

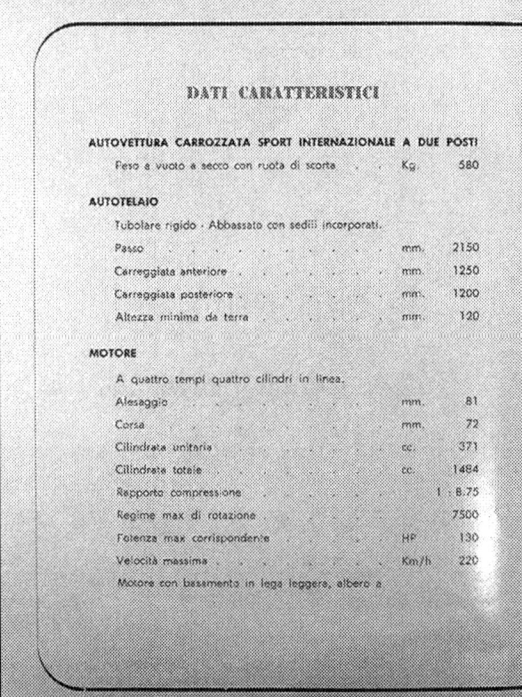

Page 2:
Background - white
DATI CARATTERISTICI - red
Print - dark blue
Border - dark blue

Competition Cars	section 6-4	cover
88 **TIPO 150/S - 1500 cc**		
blue and white folder	8⅝ x 6¼"	22 x 16 cm	Italian	Style 1

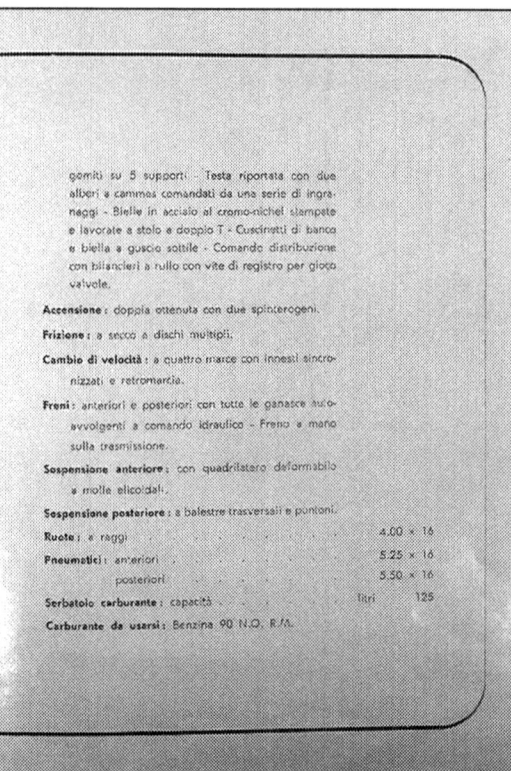

Page 3:
Background - white
Print - dark blue
Border - dark blue
Vertical stripes - red

Page 4:
Background - white
Maserati badge - blue and red

Marked:
None

Version #1: Hp 130 Rapporto Compressione 1:8.75
Version #2: Hp 140 Rapporto Compressione 1:9.25

Competition Cars	section 6-5

TIPO 200/S 2000 cc - 2-56

blue and white folder	8⁵/₈ x 6¹/₄"	22 x 16 cm	Italian	Style 1

Cover:
Background - white
Maserati badge - blue and red
MASERATI - red
Print - dark blue

Page 2:
Background - white
DATI CARATTERISTICI - red
Print - dark blue
Border - dark blue

Page 3:
Background - white
Print - dark blue
Border - dark blue
Vertical Stripes - red

Page 4:
Background - white
Maserati Badge - blue and red

Marked
500-2-56 Stab. Pol. Artioli - Modena

Competition Cars	section 6-6	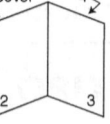
TIPO 200/SI 2000 cc - 9-56		
blue and white folder	8⁵/₈ x 6¹/₄" 22 x 16 cm Italian	Style 1

90

Cover:
Background - white
Maserati badge - blue and red
Maserati - red
Print - dark blue

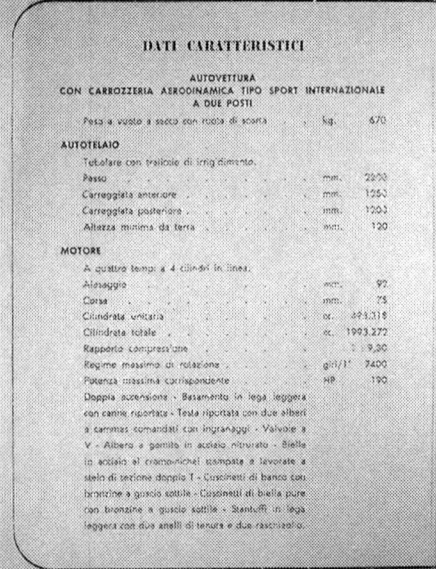

Page 2:
Background - white
DATI CARATTERISTICI - red
Print - dark blue
Border - dark blue

Competition Cars			section 6-6	cover
TIPO 200/SI 2000 cc - 9-56				91
blue and white folder	8⅝ x 6¼"	22 x 16 cm	Italian	Style 1

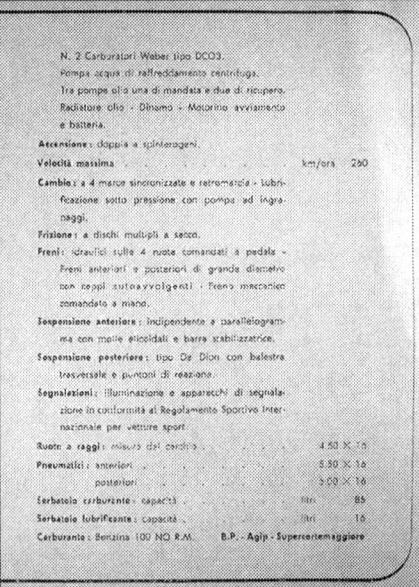

Page 3:
Background - white
Print - dark blue
Border - dark blue
Vertical stripes - red

Page 4:
Background - white
Maserati badge - blue and red

Marked
500-9-56-Stab. Pol. Artioli - Modena

Competition Cars			section 6-7	
92	**SPORT 200 SI**			
colored sheet	7³/₄ x 11⁵/₈"	19.8 x 29.6 cm	ITL, FRA, ENG	Style 2A

Front:
Background - yellow
Maserati badge - blue, red on white
Car - black and white photo
Print - black on white stripe

Rear:
Background - white
Top headings - red
Maserati badges - yellow
OFFICINE ALFIERI MASERATI
S.p.A. - red
Print - black

Marked
Stab. Pol. Artioli - Modena

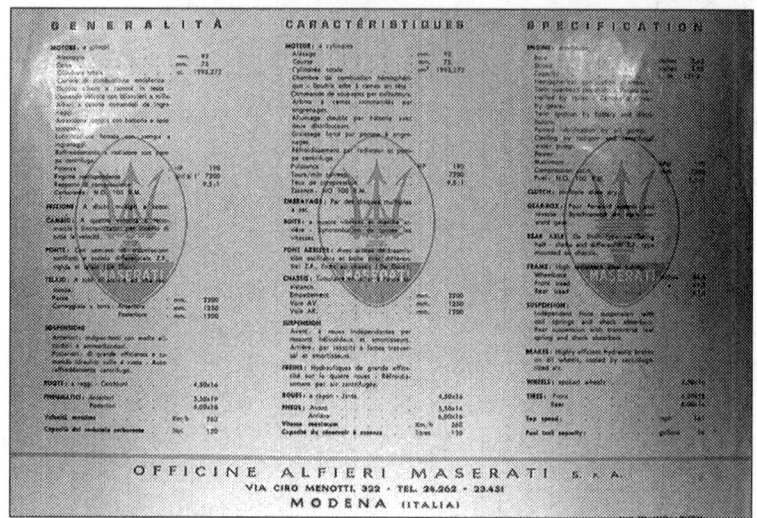

Competition Cars	section 6-8	

SPORT 200 SI - 3-57, 10-57 (REPRINTED)

1, 2 color sheet original	8¹/₁₆ x 11³/₄"	20.5 x 29.9 cm	ITL, FRA, ENG	Style 2A
3 color sheet reprint	8¹/₈ x 11¹¹/₁₆"	20.7 x 29.7 cm		

Front:
Background - yellow
Maserati badge - blue, red on white
Car - black and white photo
Print - black on white stripe

Rear:
Background - white
Top Headings - red
Maserati Badge - yellow
Print - black
OFFICINE ALFIERI MASERATI S.p.A. - red

Marked:
1. 1000-3/57 - Stab. Pol. Artioli - Modena 8¹/₁₆ x 11³/₄"
2. 1000-10/57 - Stab. Pol. Artioli - Modena 8¹/₁₆ x 11³/₄"
3. 1998 Archivio Maserati riproduzione anastatica (rear, lower left)
Printed on heavier paper. Marked 1000 - 3/57 - Stab. Pol. Artioli - Modena 8¹/₈ x 11¹¹/₁₆"

Competition Cars

TIPO 250/S - 6-54*

| blue line sheet | 11 x 8⁹/₁₆" | 28 x 21.8 cm | Italian | Style 2B |

section 6-9

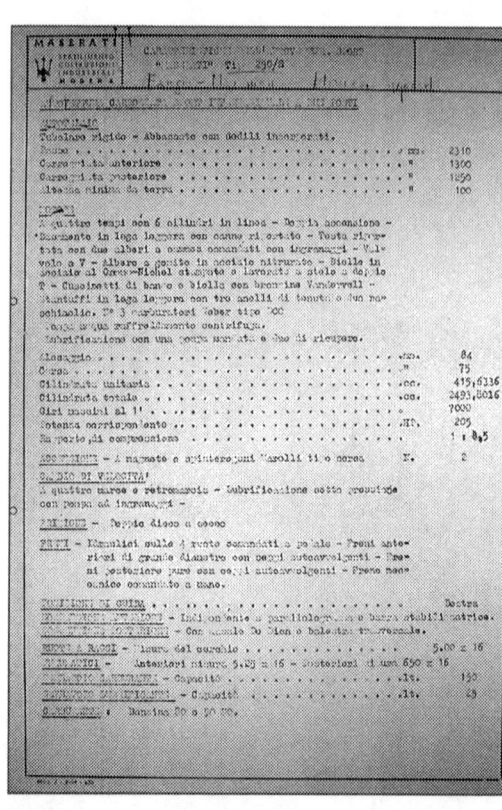

Front:
Background - white
Print - blue

Marked:
Mod. 7-6-54-635

Rear:
Background - white
Blank

*NOTE: MANY DIFFERENT ONE SIDED "BLUE LINE" PAGES ISSUED AS NEEDED.

Competition Cars			section 6-10		95
TIPO 250/F - FORMULA 1*					
blue line sheet	11 x 8⁹/₁₆"	28 x 21.8 cm	Italian	Style 2B	

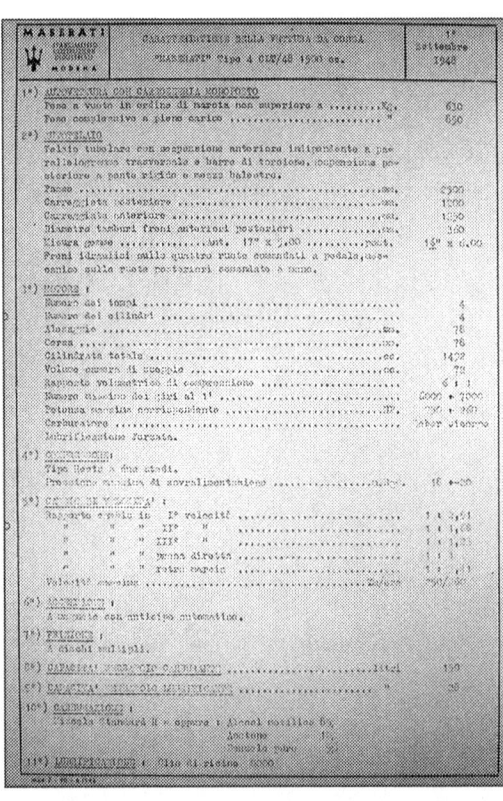

Front:
(Sheet 1)
Background - white
Print - blue

Rear:
Background - white
Blank

Marked:
A4-210-297-Mod 7

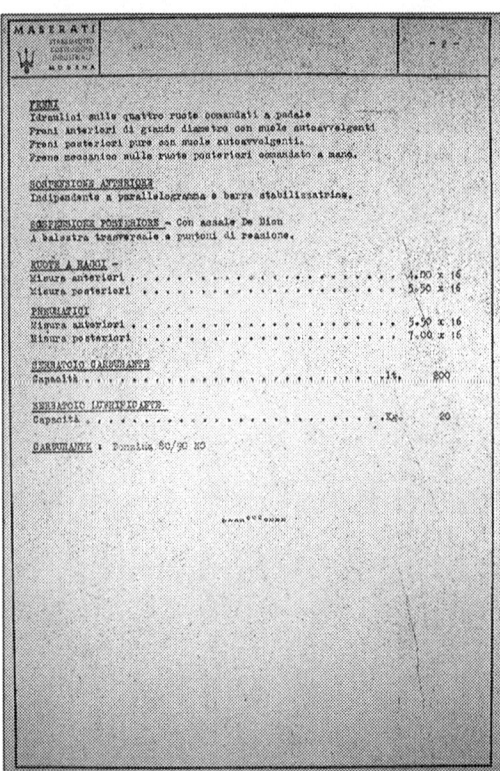

Front:
(Sheet 2)
Background - white
Print - blue

Marked:
A4-210-297-Mod. 7

Rear:
Background - white
Blank

*NOTE: MANY DIFFERENT ONE SIDED "BLUE LINE" PAGES ISSUED AS NEEDED.

Competition Cars		section 6-11	
96 LA NUOVA VETTURA MASERATI SPORT 3000 cc			
sheet	12½ x 8⅝" / 31.7 x 22 cm	Italian	Style 2B

Front:
Background - white
Maserati badge - blue and red
Car - black and white photo
Heading "La nuova" - red
Print - black

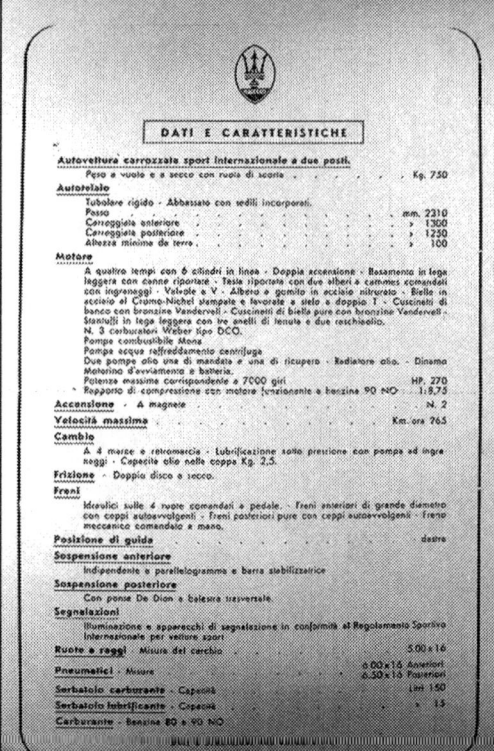

Rear:
Background - white
Maserati badge - blue and red
Border - blue
DATIE CARATTERISTICHE - red
Print - black

Marked:
Stab. Pol. Artioli - Modena

Competition Cars

section 6-12

TIPO 300/S - 6-54*

| blue line sheet | 11 x 8⁹/₁₆" | 28 x 21.8 cm | Italian | Style 2B |

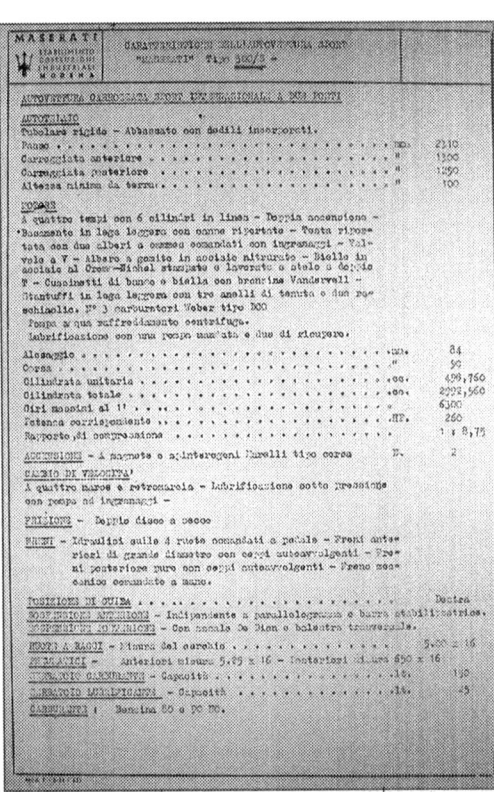

Front:
Background - white
Print - blue

Marked:
Mod. 7-6-54-635

Rear:
Background - white
Blank

*NOTE: MANY DIFFERENT ONE SIDED "BLUE LINE" PAGES ISSUED AS NEEDED.

Competition Cars

TIPO 300/S - 3-55*

| blue line sheet | 11 x 8⁹/₁₆" | 28 x 21.8 cm | Italian | Style 2B |

section 6-13

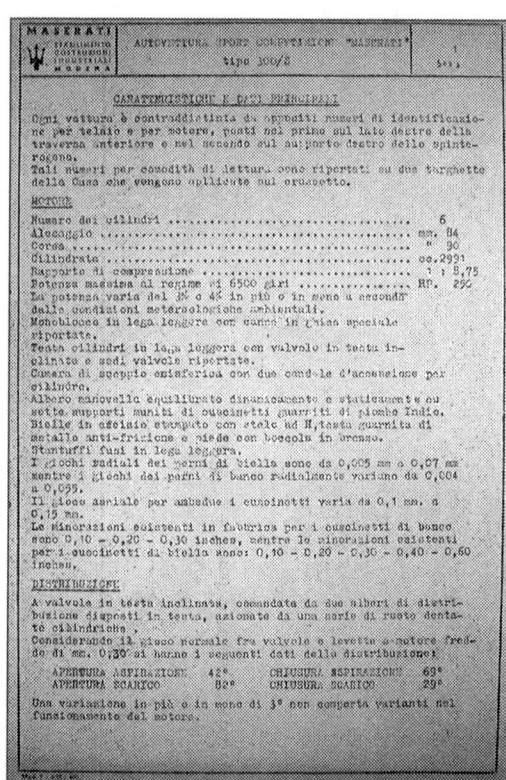

Front:
(sheet 1)
Background - white
Print - blue

Marked:
Mod. 7 - 3 - 55 - 400

Rear:
Background - white
Blank

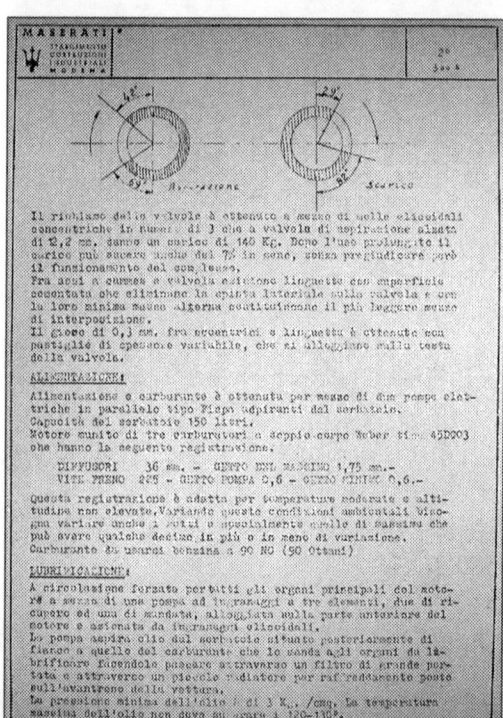

Front:
(sheet 2)
Background - white
Print - blue

Marked:
Mod. 7 - 3 - 55 - 400

Rear:
Background - white
Blank

*NOTE: MANY DIFFERENT ONE SIDED "BLUE LINE" PAGES ISSUED AS NEEDED.

Competition Cars			section 6-13	
TIPO 300/S - 3-55*				
blue line sheet	11 x 8⁹/₁₆"	28 x 21.8 cm	Italian	Style 2B

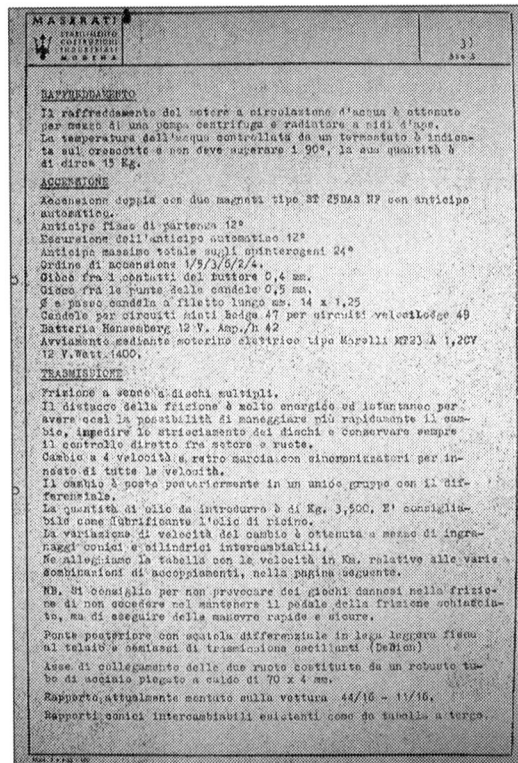

Front:
(Sheet 3)
Background - white
Print - blue

Marked:
Mod. 7 - 3 - 55 - 400

Rear:
Background - white
Blank

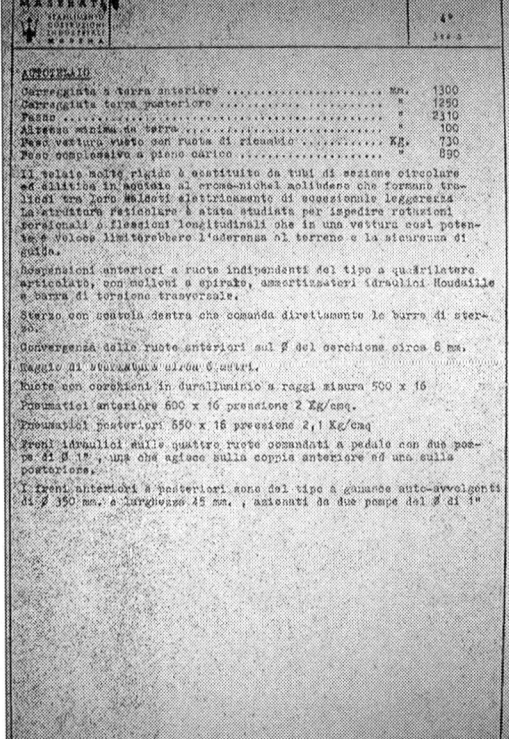

Front:
(Sheet 4)
Background - white
Print - blue

Marked:
Mod. 7 - 3 - 55 - 400

Rear:
Background - white
Blank

100	Competition Cars	section 6-14	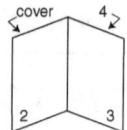

TIPO 300/S - 3000cc - 2-56

| blue and white folder | 8⅝ x 6¼" | 22 x 16 cm | Italian | Style 1 |

Cover:
Background - white
Maserati badge - blue and red
Maserati - red
Print - dark blue

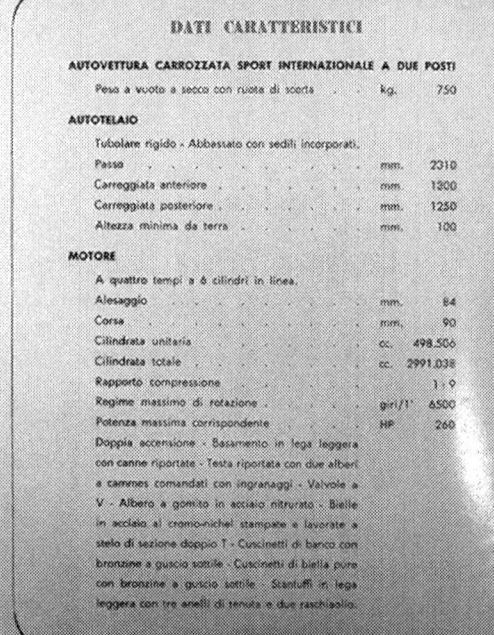

Page 2:
Background - white
DATI CARATTERISTICI - red
Print - dark blue
Border - dark blue

Competition Cars

TIPO 300/S - 3000cc - 2-56

| blue and white folder | 8⁵/₈ x 6¹/₄" | 22 x 16 cm | Italian | Style 1 |

section 6-14

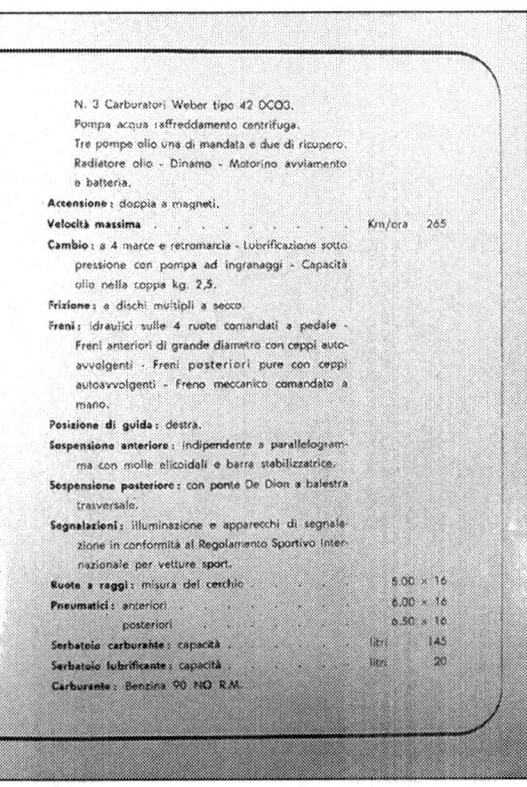

Page 3:
Background - white
Print - dark blue
Border - dark blue

Page 4:
Background - white
Maserati badge - blue and red

Marked:
No Date (Hp 245)
500-2-56 (Hp 260) Stab. Pol. Artioli - Modena

Competition Cars	section 6-15	
SPORT 300S (REPRINTED)		
1 colored sheets original 8¹/₈ x 11⁵/₈" 19.8 x 29.6 cm	ITA, FRA, ENG	Style 2A
2 colored sheets reprinted 8¹/₈ x 11¹¹/₁₆" 20.7 x 29.7 cm		

102

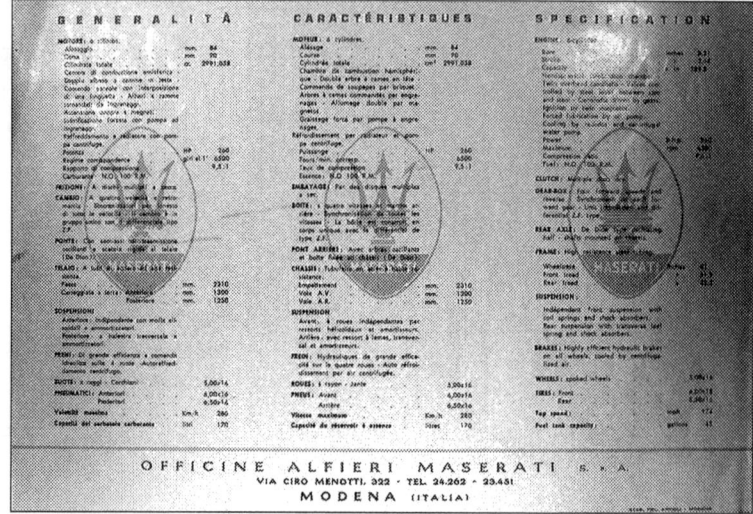

Front:
Background - pink
Maserati badge - blue and red on white
Car - black and white photo
Print - black on white stripe

Rear:
Background: white
Top headings - red
Maserati badges - pink
OFFICINE ALFIERI MASERATI
S.p.A. - red
Print - black

Marked:
1. Stab. Pol. Artioli - Modena 8¹/₈ x 11⁵/₈"
2. 1998 Archivio Maserati riproduzione anastatica (Heavier paper)
(Rear Background - grey) (Marked Rear, Lower Left) 8¹/₈ x 11¹¹/₁₆"

Competition Cars	section 6-16	
SPORT 300S - 6-57, 10-57		103
colored sheet	8¹/₈ x 11³/₄" 20.7 x 29.9 cm ITA, FRA, ENG	Style 2A

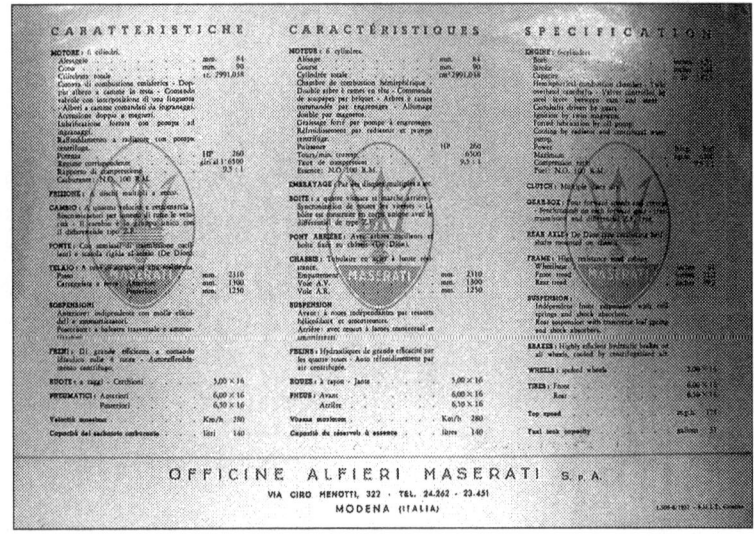

Front:
Background - pink
Maserati Badge - blue and red on white
Car - black and white photo
Print - black on white stripe

Rear:
Background - white
Top Headings - red
Maserati badge - pink
OFFICINE ALFIERI MASERATI
S.p.A. - red
Print - black

Marked:
1. 1500 - 6/1957 - S.M.I.T. - Cassino
2. 1000 - 10/57

104	**Competition Cars**	section 6-17	
	SPORT 450/S		
	1 color sheet original 2 color sheet reprint	8 x 11⁵⁄₈" 8¹⁄₈ x 11¹¹⁄₁₆"	20.4 x 29.6 cm 20.7 x 29.8 cm	ITA, FRA, ENG	Style 2A

Front:
Background - medium green
Maserati badge - blue and red on white
Car - black and white photo
Print - black on white stripe

Rear:
Background - white
Top Headings - red
Maserati badge - medium green
OFFICINE ALFIERI MASERATI
S.p.A: red
Print - black

Marked:
1. Stab. Pol. Artioli - Modena 8 x 11⁵⁄₈"
2. 1998 Archivio Maserati riproduzione anastatica (heavier paper)
(Rear Background - grey) (Rear lower left) 8¹⁄₈ x 11¹¹⁄₁₆"

Competition Cars	section 6-18		105

SPORT 450/S - 6-57, 10-57 (REPRINTED)

1, 2 colored sheet original	8¹/₈ x 11¹¹/₁₆"	20.7 x 29.7 cm	ITA, FRA, ENG	Style 2A
3 colored sheet reprint	8¹/₁₆ x 11³/₄"	20.5 x 29.9 cm		

Front:
Background - medium green
Maserati badge - blue and red on white
Car - black and white photo
Print - black on white stripe

Rear:
Background - white
Top headings - red
Maserati badges - medium green
OFFICINE ALFIERI MASERATI
S.p.A. - red
Print - black

Marked:
1. 1500 - 6 - 1957 - S.M.I.T. Cassino 8¹/₈ x 11¹¹/₁₆"
2. 1000 - 10/1957 S.M.I.T. Cassino
3. 1000 - 10/1957 - S.M.I.T. Cassino RPI 2017-1988 (Australia) 8¹/₁₆ x 11³/₄"

CARATTERISTICHE DELLE NUOVA VENTURE SPORT MASERATI - 4 CILINDRI TIPO 60, TIPO 61*

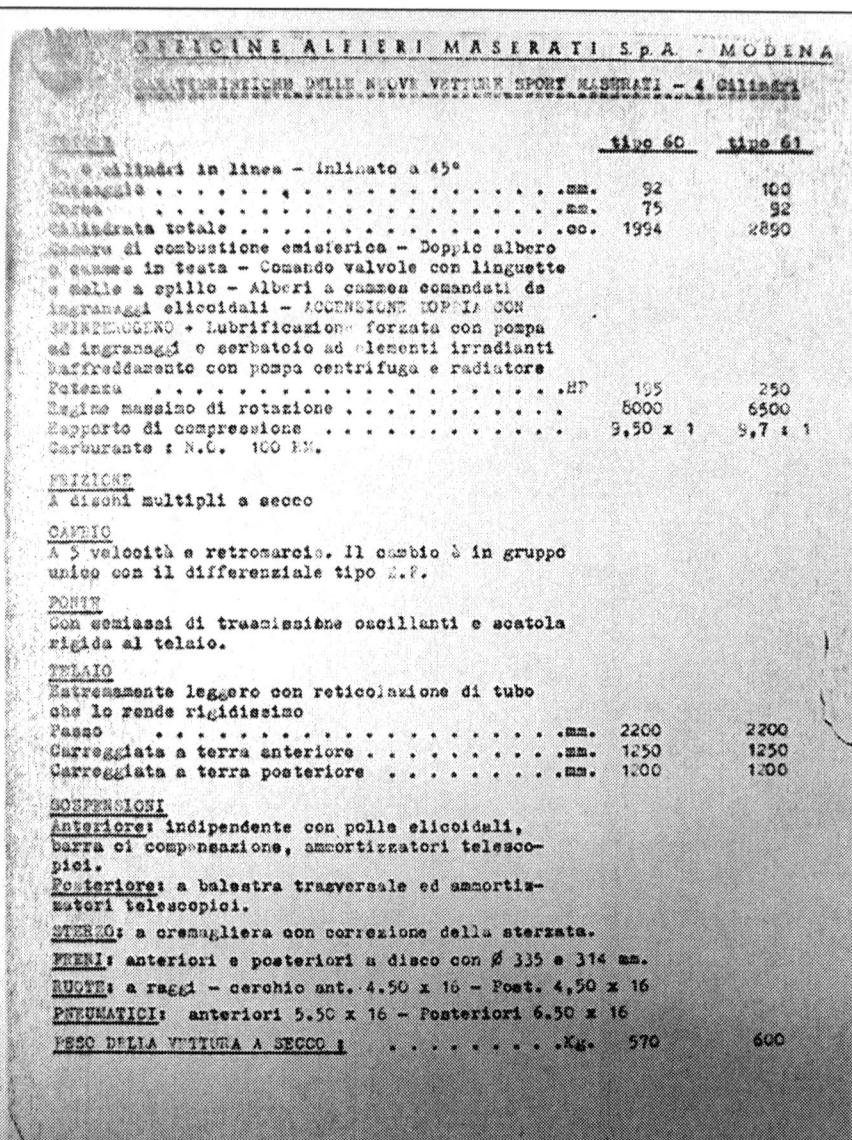

Competition Cars	section 6-20	
VETTURETTA MASERATI TIPO SPORT		107
blue line sheet	11 x 8⁹/₁₆"	28 x 21.8 cm	Italian	Style 2B

VETTURETTA MASERATI Tipo Sport

POSTI : 2 affiancati
TRAZIONE : Elettrica a mezzo di batteria e motorino collegato all'asse posteriore
MARCIA : Avanti e indietro comandata a mezzo di leva posta sul cruscotto a lato sinistro del volante. Le posizioni sono definite dallo schizzo a fianco.
REGOLAZIONE DI VELOCITA' : A mezzo di acceleratore a pedale sul lato destro.
VELOCITA' MASSIMA : 12 Km/h
AUTONOMIA : Quattro ore e mezzo di marcia con una carica di batteria
BATTERIA : 53 Amp/h alloggiata sull'avantreno. 12 Volt.
CONSUMO : In marcia circa 12 Amp/h
CARICA BATTERIA : Si esegue direttamente sui morsetti scoprendo il cofano anteriore. Si consiglia la carica a tipo lento per la migliore conservazione e durata della batteria.
FRENI : A pedale sul lato sinistro dell'acceleratore. A mano con leva posta sul lato destro del pilota. Il freno a ganasce e tamburo è posto sulla ruota posteriore destra.
SOSPENSIONI : Indipendenti sulle quattro ruote con molle elicoidali
RAGGIO MINIMO DI STERZATA : metri 2 , 50
DIMENSIONI D'INGOMBRO : Lunghezza mt. 2 - Larghezza mt.0,78 - Altezza mt. 0,48 .
ILLUMINAZIONE : 2 Fanali anteriori e fanale posteriore , comandati da interuttore posto sul cruscotto sul lato destro del volante.
PNEUMATICI : Con camera d'aria - Dimensioni 12"x1½"x2 1/4"
RUOTE : Fissate con galletti e quattro prigionieri
PESO : Con batteria Kg. 75

Front:
Background - white
Print - blue

Rear:
Background - white
Blank

Marked:
Mod. 7-9-56-500

*NOTE: MANY DIFFERENT ONE SIDED "BLUE LINE" PAGES ISSUED AS NEEDED.

This was a limited production of a childs two seater. Adolfo Orsi shown "driving."

From the collection of Dr. Adolfo Orsi.

3500 GT - TIPO 101 1957-1964

GRAN TURISMO 3500 - ALEMANO COUPE	7-1
GRAN TURISMO 3500 - FEATURES - 500 - 3/57	7-2
GRAN TURISMO 3500 - LINE DRAWINGS -1500 - 3/57	7-3
GRAN TURISMO 3500 ZAGATO COUPE - 500 - 3/57	7-4
GRAN TURISMO 3500 - TOURING COUPE - 1000 - 3/57	7-5
GRAN TURISMO 3500 - ALEMANO COUPE - 500 - 3/57	7-6
GRAN TURISMO 3500 - ALEMANO COUPE - 1.500 - 6/1957	7-7
GRAN TURISMO 3500 - TOURING COUPE - 1.500 - 6/1957	7-8
GRAN TURISMO 3500/T - TOURING COUPE - 1000 - 12/1957	7-9
3500 GT	7-10
3500 GT	7-11
3500 GT - 1960	7-12
3500 GT - 1960	7-13
3500 GT - 10.000 4/60	7-14
3500 GT - 1961	7-15
3500 GT - 5000 - 7/61	7-16
3500 GT A CARBURATORI 3500 GT A INIEZIONE	7-17

3500 GT - TIPO 101

3500 GT A CARBURATORI 3500 GT A INIEZIONE	7-18
3500 G.T. - A CARBURATORI - A INIEZIONE (REPRINTED)	7-19
3500 G.T. CARBURATORI INIEZIONE	7-20
VETTURA MASERATI 3500 GT A CARBURATORI	7-21
3500 GT A INIEZIONE	7-22
3500 G.T. WITH CARBURETTORS	7-23
MASERATI 3500 G.T. FUEL INJECTION	7-24
3500 GT SPYDER	7-25
3500 GT SPYDER - 1961	7-26
3500 GT BERLINA ANNO 1960 OMOLOGATO SHEET	7-27
TOWN & COUNTRY REPRINT	7-28

3500 GT - TIPO 101

GRAN TURISMO 3500 - ALEMANO COUPE

| color sheet | 8 x 11⁵⁄₈" | 20.4 x 29.6 cm | ITA, FRA, ENG | Style 2A |

Front:
Background - orange
Car - black and white photo
Print - black on white stripe
Maserati badge - blue and red on white

Rear:
Background - white
Top headings - red
Maserati badges - orange
OFFICINE ALFIERI MASERATI
S.p.A. - red
Print - black

Marked:
STAB. POL. ARTIOLI - MODENA

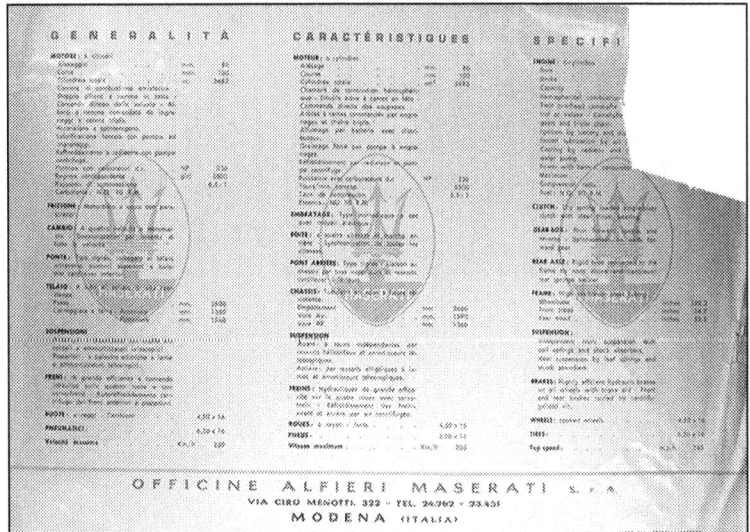

3500 GT - TIPO 101			section 7-2	
112	**GRAN TURISMO 3500 - FEATURES - 500 - 3/57**			
	color sheet	8 x 11⅝" · 20.4 x 29.6 cm	Italian	Style 2A

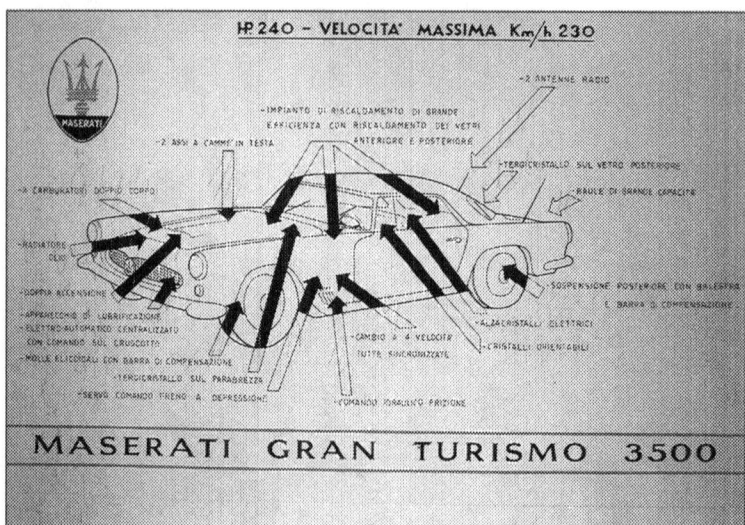

Front:
Background - white
Maserati badge - blue and red
2 horizontal thin stripes - red
Car, Arrows and Print - dark blue

Rear:
Background - white
Car - grey and white photo
Engine and chassis cutaways - red
OFFICINE ALFIERI MASERATI S.p.A. - red
Horizontal stripe - grey
Print - dark blue

Marked:
500 - 3/57 - STAB. POL. ARTIOLI

3500 GT - TIPO 101

GRAN TURISMO 3500 - LINE DRAWINGS - 1500 - 3/57

| sheet | 8¹/₁₆ x 11¹¹/₁₆" | 20.6 x 29.8 cm | ITA, FRA, ENG | Style 2A |

section 7-3

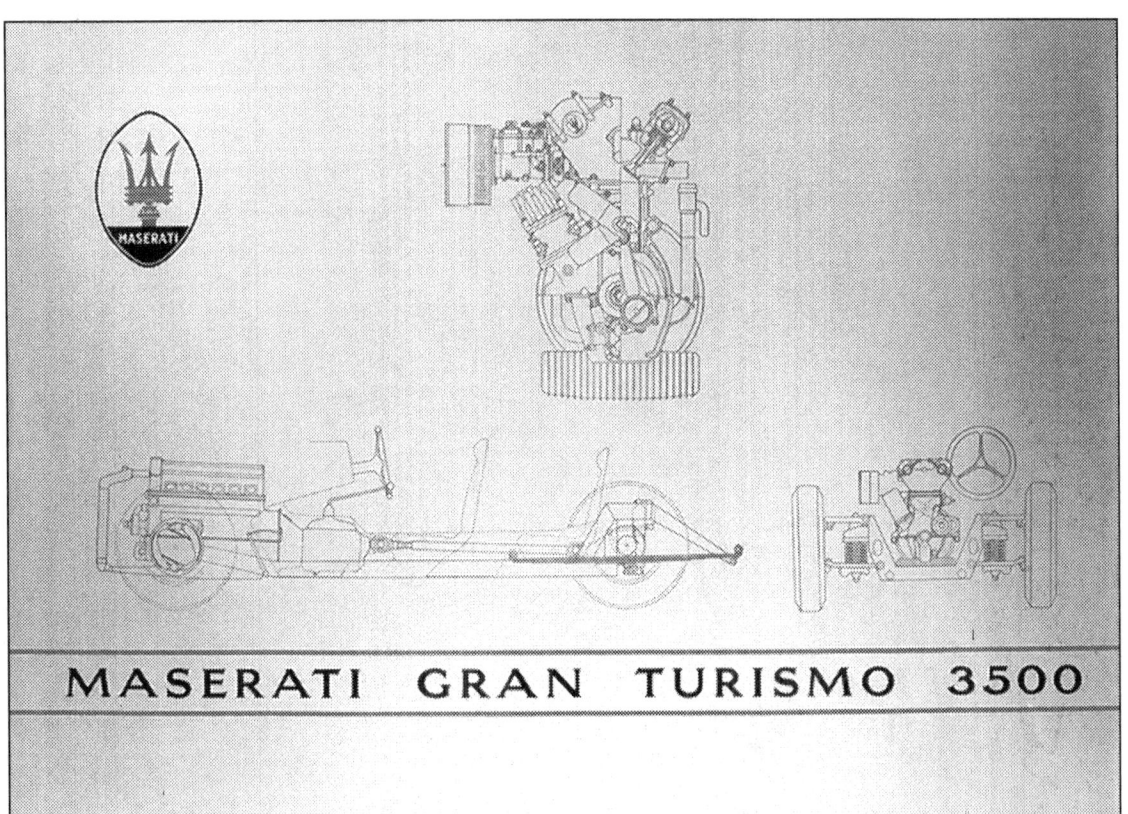

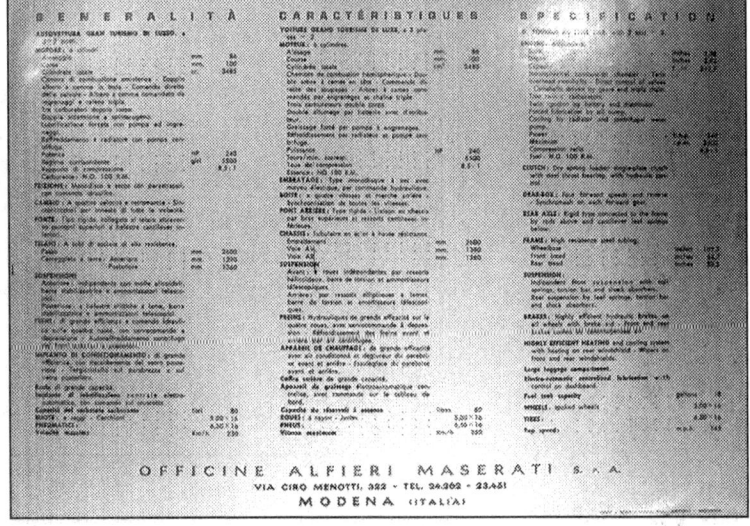

Front:
Background - white
Maserati badge - blue and red
Cutaways - red
Horizontal stripes - red
Print - black

Rear:
Background - white
Top headings - red
OFFICINE ALFIERI MASERATI
S.p.A. - red
Print - black

Marked:
1500 - 3/57 - STAB. POL.
ARTIOLI - MODENA

3500 GT - TIPO 101	section 7-4	
GRAN TURISMO 3500 - ZAGATO COUPE - 500 - 3/57		
color sheet	8 1/16 x 11 5/8" 20.5 x 29.6 cm	ITA, FRA, ENG	Style 2A

Front:
Background - brick red
Maserati badge - blue and red on white
Car - black and white illustration
Print - black on white stripe

Rear:
Background - white
Top headings - brick red
Maserati badges - brick red
OFFICINE ALFIERI MASERATI
S.p.A. - red
Print - black

Marked:
500 - 3/57 - STAB. POL.
ARTIOLI - MODENA

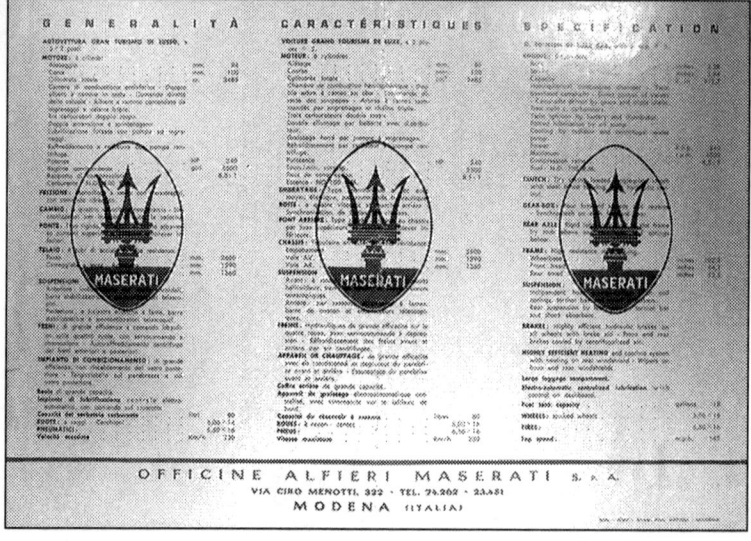

3500 GT - TIPO 101

GRAN TURISMO 3500 - TOURING COUPE - 1000 - 3/57

| color sheet | 8¹/₁₆ x 11⁵/₈" | 20.5 x 29.6 cm | ITA, FRA, ENG | Style 2A |

section 7-5

Front:
Background - blue / grey
Maserati badge - blue and red on white
Car - black and white illustration
Touring badge - dark blue
Print - black on white stripe

Rear:
Background - white
Top headings - red
Maserati badges - blue / grey
OFFICINE ALFIERI MASERATI
S.p.A. - red
Print - black

Marked:
1000 - 3/57 - STAB. POL. ARTIOLI - MODENA

3500 GT - TIPO 101

GRAN TURISMO 3500 - ALEMANO COUPE - 500 - 3/57

section 7-6

| color sheet | 8¹/₁₆ x 11⁵/₈" | 20.6 x 29.6 cm | ITA, FRA, ENG | Style 2A |

Front:
Background - grey
Maserati badge - blue and red on white
Car - black and white illustration
Print - black on white stripe

Rear:
Background - white
Top headings - red
Masterati badges - grey
OFFICINE ALFIERI MASERATI
S.p.A. - red
Print - black

Marked:
500 - 3/57 - STAB. POL.
ARTIOLI - MODENA

3500 GT - TIPO 101

GRAN TURISMO 3500 - ALEMANO COUPE - 1.500 - 6/1957

| color sheet | 8¹/₈ x 11³/₄ " | 20.7 x 29.8 cm | ITA, FRA, ENG | Style 2A |

section 7-7

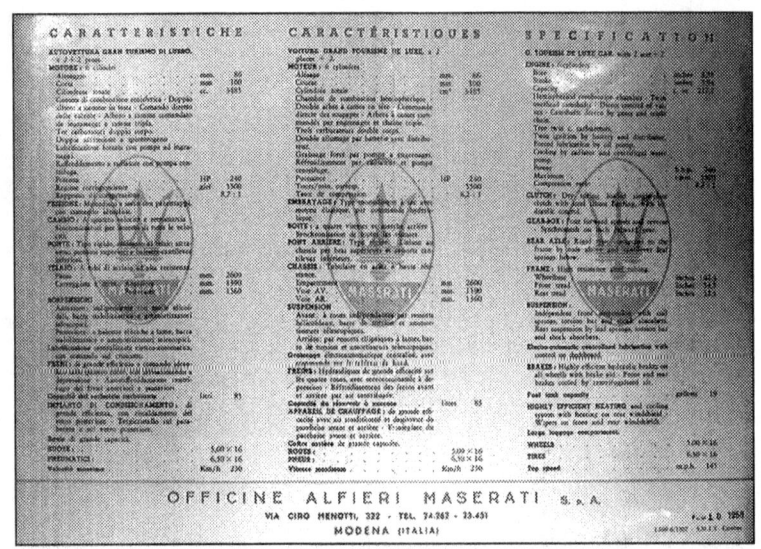

Front:
Background - putty
Maserati badge - blue and red on white
Car - black and white photo
Print - black on white stripe

Rear:
Background - white
Top headings - red
Maserati badges - putty
OFFICINE ALFIERI MASERATI
S.p.A. - red
Print - black

Marked:
1. 500 - 6/1957 - S.M.I.T. Cassino

3500 GT - TIPO 101 — section 7-8

GRAN TURISMO 3500 - TOURING COUPE - 1.500 - 6/1957

| color sheet | 8 1/8 x 11 3/4" | 20.7 x 29.7 cm | ITA, FRA, ENG | Style 2A |

Front:
Background - grey
Maserati badge - blue and red on white
Car - black and white photo
Print - black on white stripe

Rear:
Background - white
Top headings - red
Maserati badges - grey
OFFICINE ALFIERI MASERATI S.p.A. - red
Print - black

Marked:
1.500 - 6/1957 - S.M.I.T. - Cassino

3500 GT - TIPO 101

GRAN TURISMO 3500/T - TOURING COUPE - 1000 - 12/1957

| colored sheet | 8¼ x 11¹³⁄₁₆ " | 21 x 30 cm | ITA, FRA, ENG | Style 2A |

section 7-9

Front:
Background - grey
Maserati badge - blue and red on white
Car - black and white photo
Print - black on white stripe

Rear:
Background - white
Top headings - red
Maserati badges - grey
OFFICINE ALFIERI MASERATI
S.p.A. - red
Print - black

Marked:
1. 1000 - 12/57 - S.M.I.T. - Cassino
2. No date SMTS - Modena

3500 GT - TIPO 101			section 7-10	
3500 GT				
color brochure	8½ x 11⅜"	21.6 x 29 cm	ITA, FRA, ENG, DEU	Style 3

Cover:
Background - white
Maserati badge - blue and red
Car - dark blue with red trident in grille
Print - medium blue on light blue stripe
Corner graphics - green, blue, red, pink and blue / grey

Page 2:
Background - white
Graph - black print
Graph - medium blue
Band - light blue with medium blue print

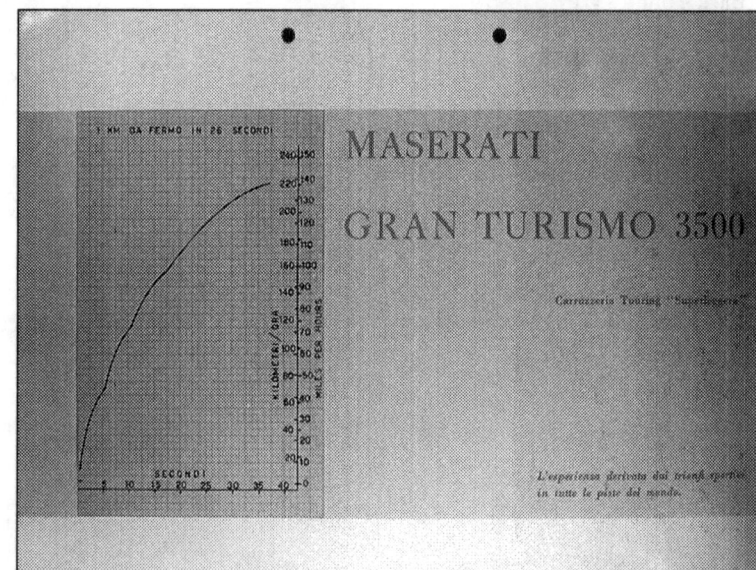

3500 GT - TIPO 101			section 7-10		121
3500 GT					
color brochure	8½ x 11⅜"	21.6 x 29 cm	ITA, FRA, ENG, DEU	Style 3	

Page 3:
Color photo - dark blue car with red trident in grille

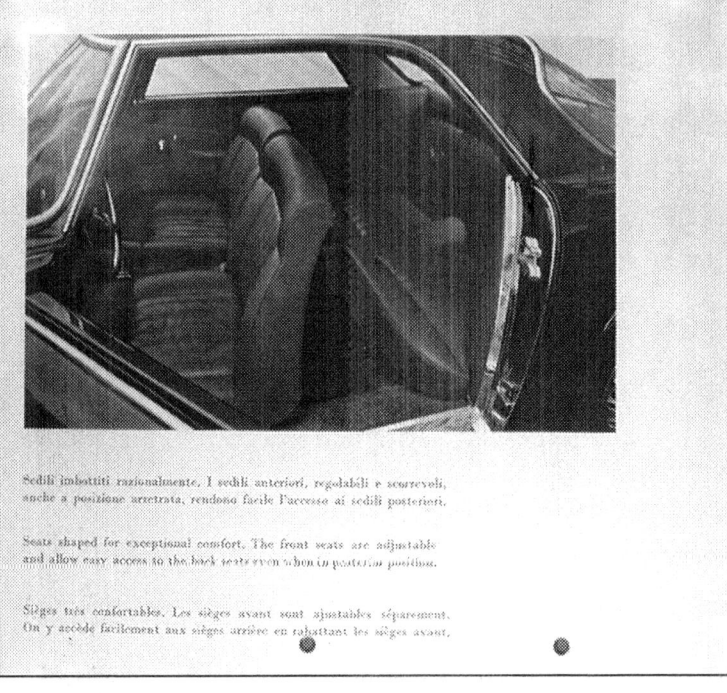

Page 4:
Background - white
Photo - dark red interior of dark blue car
Print - black
Vertical stripe - light blue

122	3500 GT - TIPO 101			section 7-10	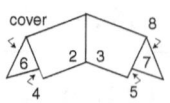
	3500 GT				
	color brochure	8½ x 11⅜"	21.6 x 29 cm	ITA, FRA, ENG, DEU	Style 3

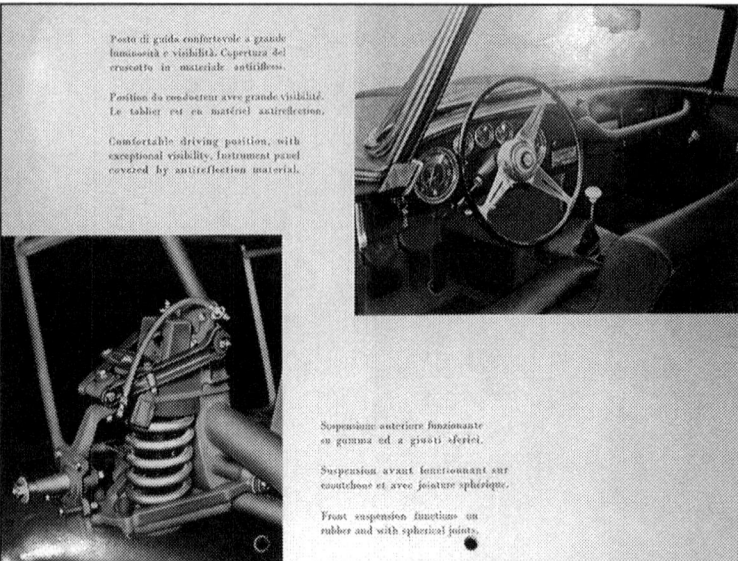

Page 5:
Background - white
Suspension - color photo of green frame and suspension
Interior - color photo, dark blue car, dark red upholstery
Print - black

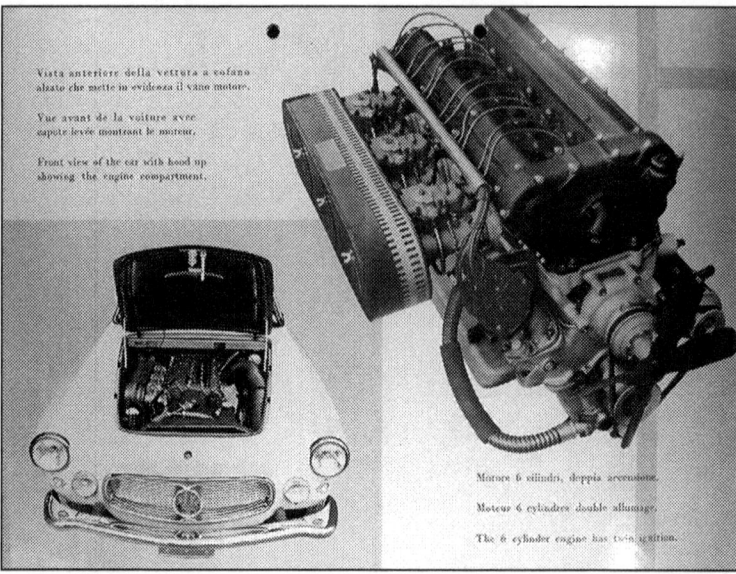

Page 6:
Background - white
Car - color photo, yellow car
Engine - tinted photo
Print - black
Stripe - light blue

3500 GT - TIPO 101			section 7-10	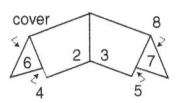	123
3500 GT					
color brochure	8½ x 11⅜"	21.6 x 29 cm	ITA, FRA, ENG, DEU	Style 3	

Page 7:
Background - white
Maserati badge - blue and red
Car - color photo, yellow car
Print - black
Stripe - blue

Page 8:
Background - white
Top headings - red
Maserati badge - blue and red
Horizontal line - blue
Print - black except company
name & address - red

Marked:
ARNOLDO MONDADORI
EDITORE - OFFICINE
GRAFICHE

3500 GT - TIPO 101			section 7-11	
3500 G.T.				
color brochure	8½ x 11³⁄₈"	21.5 x 29 cm	ITA, FRA, ENG, DEU	Style 3

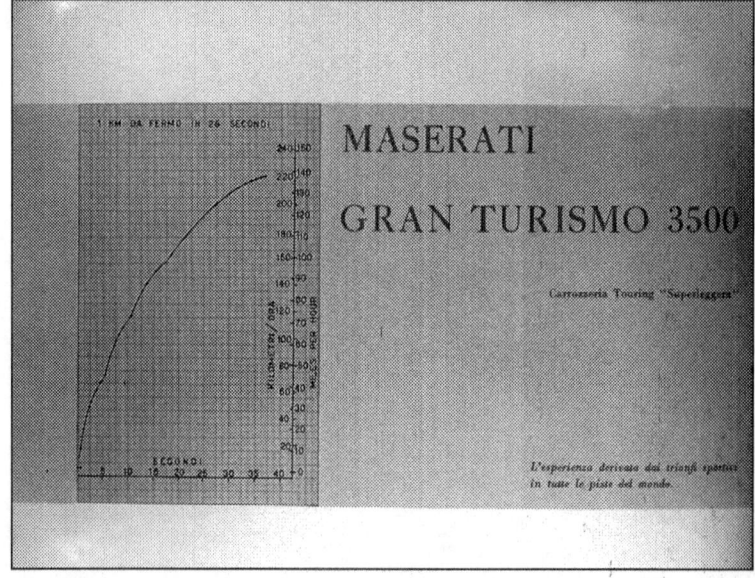

Cover:
Color photo - dark blue car on brown flagstone
Print - white outlined in black
Grass - green

Page 2:
Background - white
Graph - black print
Graph - medium blue
Band - light blue with medium blue print

3500 GT - TIPO 101			section 7-11	
3500 G.T.				
color brochure	8½ x 11³⁄₈"	21.5 x 29 cm	ITA, FRA, ENG, DEU	Style 3

Page 3:
Color photo - dark blue car with red interior
Flagstone - brown

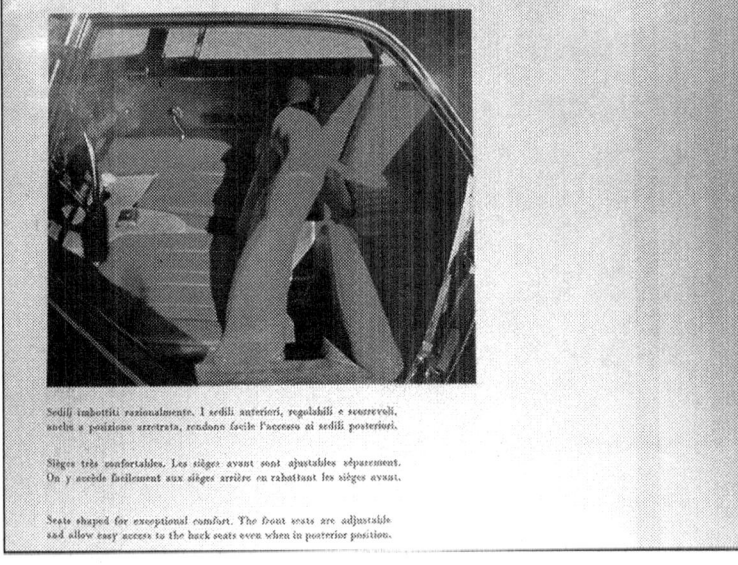

Page 4:
Background - white
Color photo - dark blue car, red interior
Print - black
Vertical stripe - yellow

126	**3500 GT - TIPO 101**	section 7-11	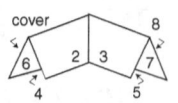
	3500 G.T.		

| color brochure | 8½ x 11³⁄₈" | 21.5 x 29 cm | ITA, FRA, ENG, DEU | Style 3 |

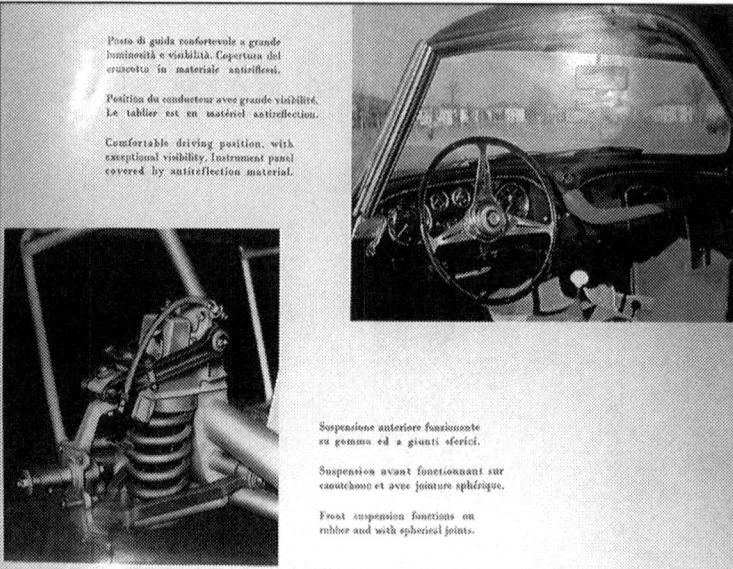

Page 5:
Background - white
Interior - color photo, dark blue car, red interior
Suspension - black and white photo
Print - black

Page 6:
Background - white
Car - dark blue
Engine - black and white photo
Print - black
Stripe - yellow

3500 GT - TIPO 101	section 7-11	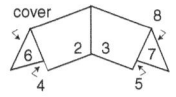
3500 G.T.		
color brochure	8½ x 11⅜"	21.5 x 29 cm	ITA, FRA, ENG, DEU	Style 3

Page 7:
Background - white
Maserati badge - blue and red
Car - dark blue
Dress - brown
Horizontal stripe - yellow
Print - black

Page 8:
Background - white
Top headings - red
Maserati badge - blue and red
Horizontal line - blue
Print - black except company
name and address - red

Marked:
ARNOLDO MONDADORI EDITORE - OFFICINE GRAFICHE

3500 GT - TIPO 101		section 7-12	
3500 GT - 1960			
colored sheet	8⁵/₁₆ x 11³/₄" / 21.3 x 29.9 cm	ITA, FRA, ENG, DEU	Style 2A

Front:
Car - black and white photo
Maserati badge & square - red
Bottom band - black
Maserati gt - white
3500 - yellow

Rear:
Background - white
Top stripe - black with white print
Bottom stripe - black
Maserati badge & square - red
Background of specifications - yellow
Print - black
10.000 - yellow

Marked:
Manelli e Rondelli STUDIO CALDERINI
10.000 - Officine Grafiche Calderini - Bologna - 1960

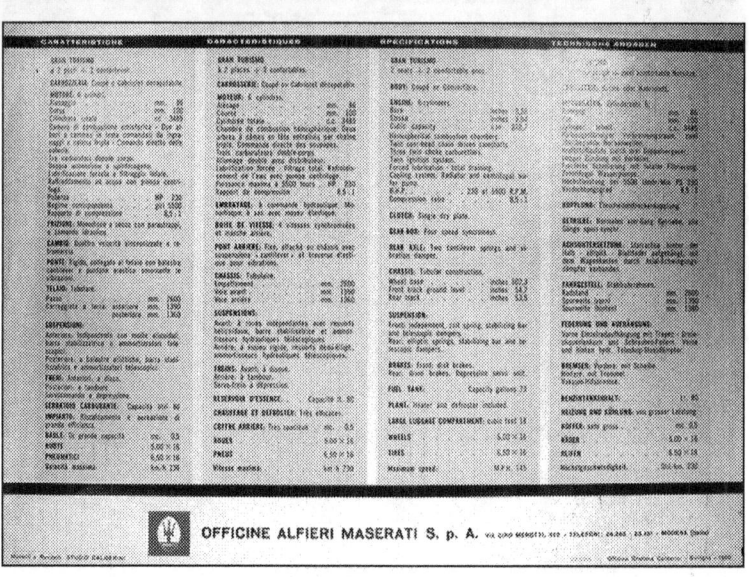

3500 GT - TIPO 101	section 7-13	
3500 GT - 1960		
color folder	8 1/8 x 11 3/8"	20.6 x 29 cm	ITA, FRA, ENG, DEU	Style 5

Cover:
Color photo - dark blue car with red interior on brown flagstone
Grass - green
Bottom band - black
Maserati gt - white
3500 - yellow

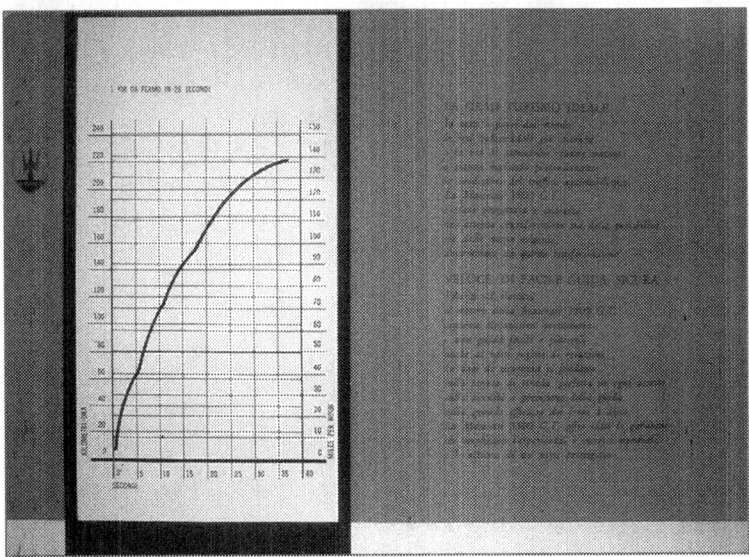

Page 2:
Background - red
Graph background - white
Print and graph border - black
Bottom band - white

130	**3500 GT - TIPO 101**			section 7-13	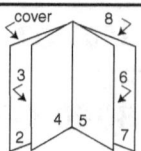
	3500 GT - 1960				
	color folder	8 1/8 x 11 3/8"	20.6 x 29 cm	ITA, FRA, ENG, DEU	Style 5

Page 3:
Color photo - dark blue car with red interior
Flagstone - brown

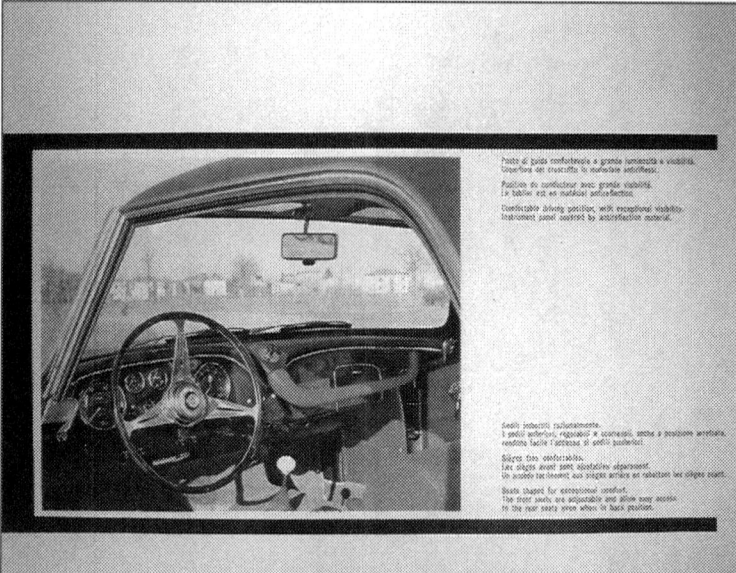

Page 4:
Background - white
Photo - dark blue car, red interior
Border - black
Print - black

3500 GT - TIPO 101			section 7-13		131
3500 GT - 1960					
color folder	8 1/8 x 11 3/8"	20.6 x 29 cm	ITA, FRA, ENG, DEU	Style 5	

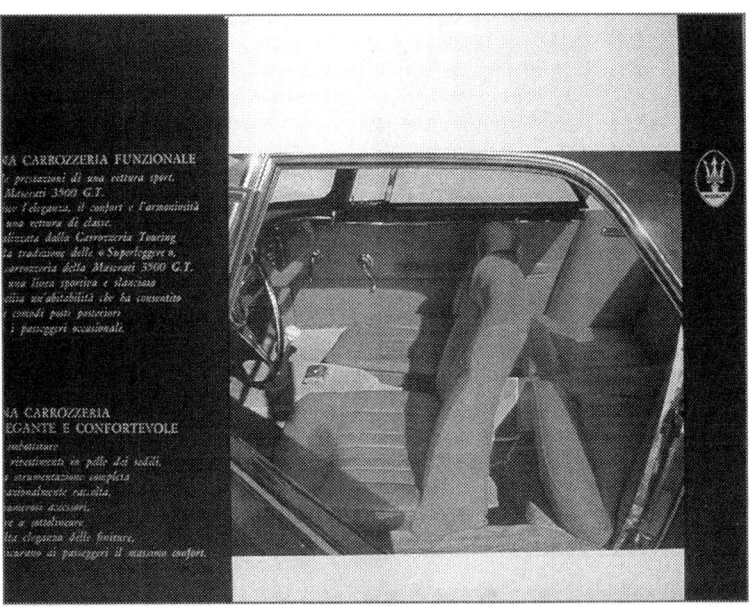

Page 5:
Color photo - dark blue car with red interior
Left/Right borders - black with white print and badge

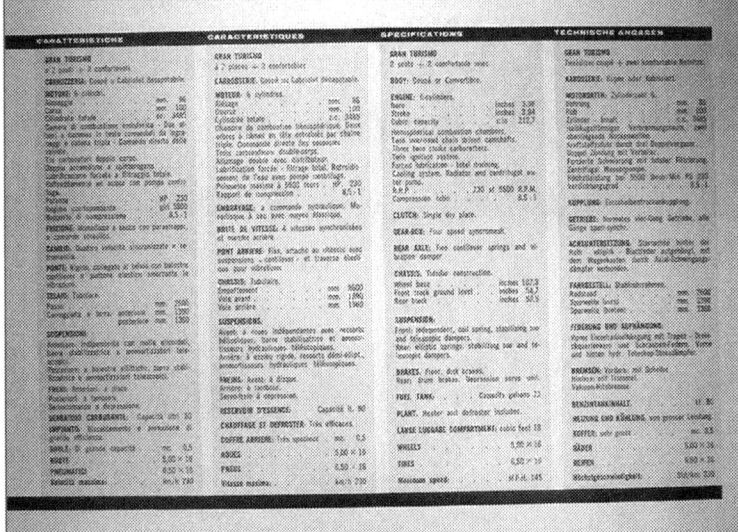

Page 6:
Background - white
Top stripe - black with white print
Bottom stripe - black
Background of specifications - yellow
Print - black

132	**3500 GT - TIPO 101**	section 7-13	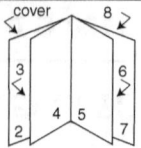
	3500 GT - 1960		
	color folder 8¹/₈ x 11³/₈" 20.6 x 29 cm ITA, FRA, ENG, DEU		Style 5

Page 7:
Background - white
Vertical bands - red
Print - black

Page 8:
Background - white
Color photo - dark blue car, brown flagstone
Left band - red
Print - black

Marked:
Officine Grafiche Calderini - Via Emilia Levante 31/2 - Bologna - 1960 Manelli e Rondelli STUDIO CALDERINI

3500 GT - TIPO 101				section 7-14	
3500 GT - 10.000 4/60					
color folder	8³/₁₆ x 11¹/₂"	21 x 29.3 cm	ITA, FRA, ENG, DEU		Style 5

Cover:
Color photo - red car, brown background
Right vertical band - black
Maserati gt - white
3500 - yellow

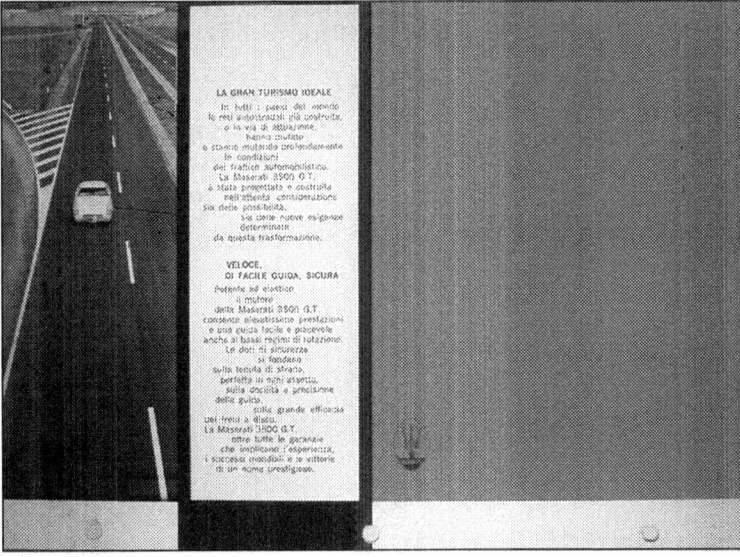

Page 2:
Background - white
Left color photo - yellow car on black road
Center border - black
Right panel - red
Print - black

134	**3500 GT - TIPO 101**	section 7-14	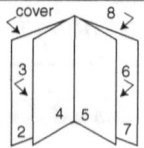
	3500 GT - 10.000 4/60		
	color folder 8³/₁₆ x 11¹/₂" 21 x 29.3 cm ITA, FRA, ENG, DEU		Style 5

Page 3:
Color photo - red car
Bottom border - black

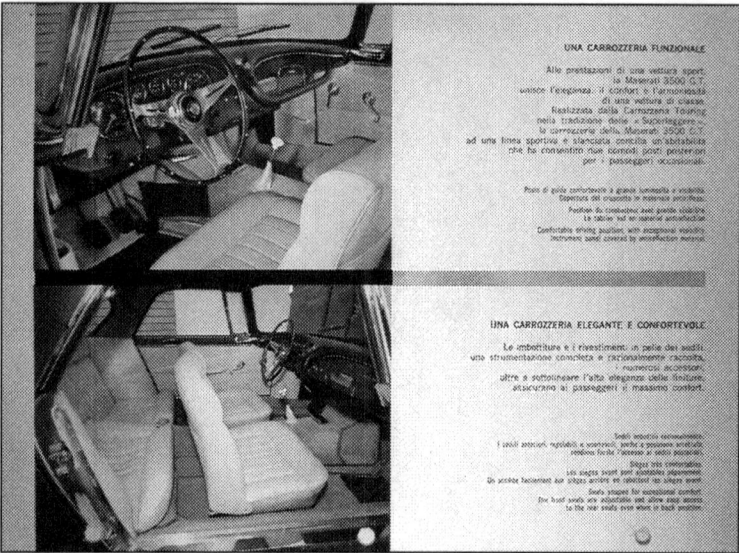

Page 4:
Background - white
Color photos - grey car with ivory interior
Center horizontal band:
    left - black
    right - grey
Print - black

3500 GT - TIPO 101			section 7-14	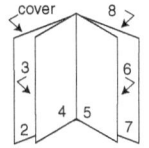	
3500 GT - 10.000 4/60					
color folder	8³/₁₆ x 11½"	21 x 29.3 cm	ITA, FRA, ENG, DEU	Style 5	

Page 5:
Color photo - dark blue car
Sky - blue
Earth - brown
Left stripe- black

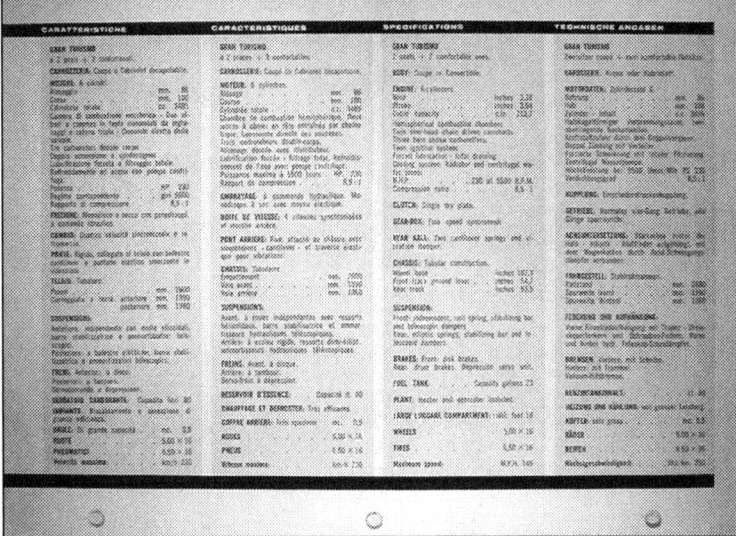

Page 6:
Background - white
Top stripe - black with white print
Bottom stripe - black
Background of specifications - yellow
Print - black

136	**3500 GT - TIPO 101**	section 7-14	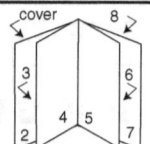
	3500 GT - 10.000 4/60		
	color folder 8³/₁₆ x 11½" 21 x 29.3 cm ITA, FRA, ENG, DEU		Style 5

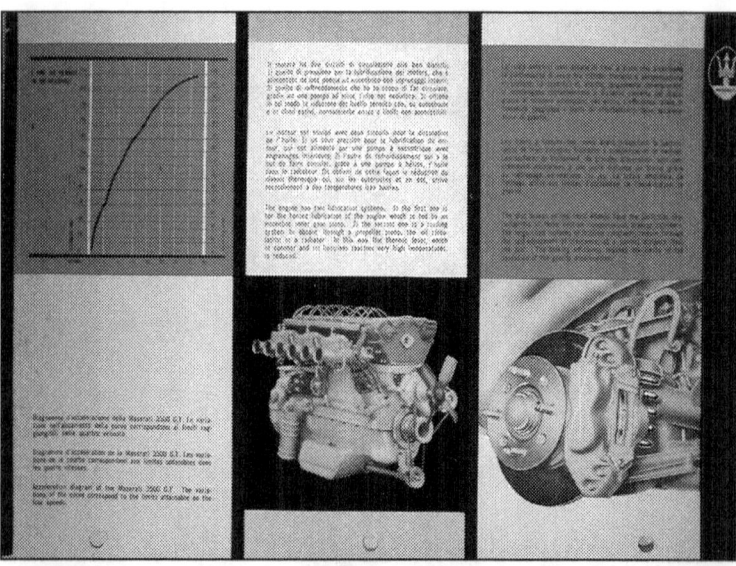

Page 7:
Background - white
Left top square: red,
    vertical lines - white,
    remainder - black
Right top square: red, print black
Engine - black and white photo tinted yellow
Suspension - black and white photo
Maserati badge - white on black band
Print - black

Page 8:
Background - white
Cars:
    left - red
    right - yellow with red interior
Left rectangle - red
Maserati badge - red on grey background
Print - black

Marked:
10.000 - 4/60 - Officine Grafiche Calderini - Bologna Studio Calderini

3500 GT - TIPO 101			section 7-15		137
3500 GT - 1961					
black and white sheet	8¼ x 11¾"	21 x 30 cm	ITA, FRA, ENG, DEU	Style 2A	

Front:
Black and white photo
Print - black on white band

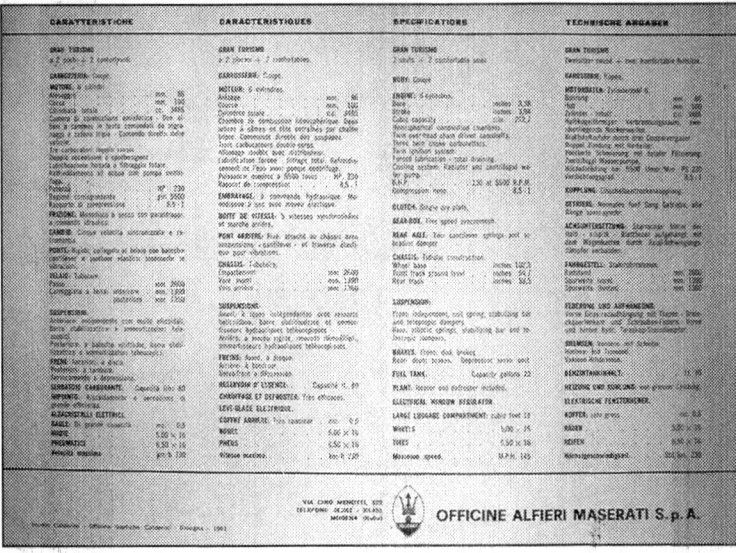

Rear:
Background - white
Print - black

Marked
Studio Calderini - Officine Grafiche Calderini - Bologna - 1961

138	**3500 GT - TIPO 101**	section 7-16	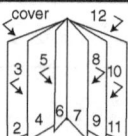
	3500 GT - 5000 - 7/61		
	color folder 8³/₁₆ x 11½" 21 x 29.3 cm ITA, FRA, ENG, DEU		Style 6

Cover:
Color photo - red car, brown background
Right vertical band - black
Maserati gt - white
3500 - yellow

Page 2:
Background - white
Left color photo - yellow car on black road
Center border - black
Right panel - red
Print - black

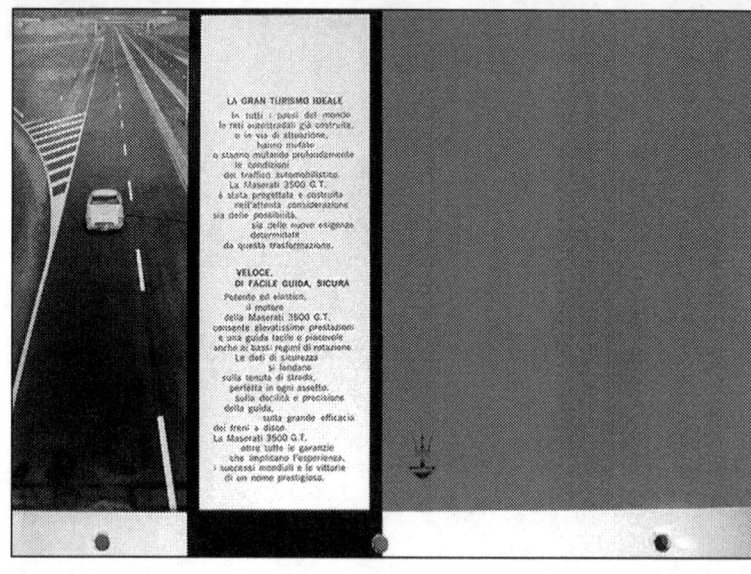

3500 GT - TIPO 101			section 7-16	
3500 GT - 5000 - 7/61				
color folder	8³/₁₆ x 11¹/₂"	21 x 29.3 cm	ITA, FRA, ENG, DEU	Style 6

Page 3:
Color photo - red car
Bottom border - black

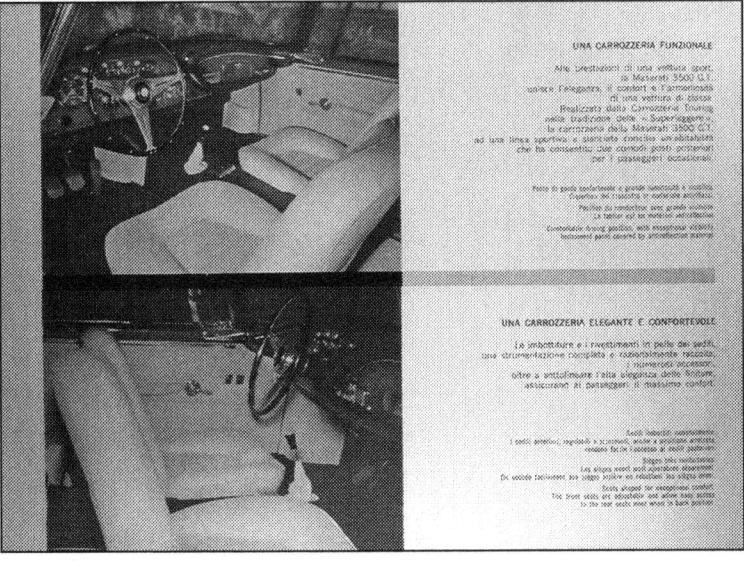

Page 4:
Background - white
Color photos - grey car
   with ivory interior
Center horizontal band -
   left - black
   right - grey
Print - black

140	**3500 GT - TIPO 101**	section 7-16	
	3500 GT - 5000 - 7/61		
	color folder	8³/₁₆ x 11¹/₂" 21 x 29.3 cm ITA, FRA, ENG, DEU	Style 6

Page 5:
Background - red
Maserati badge - black
Right vertical band - white

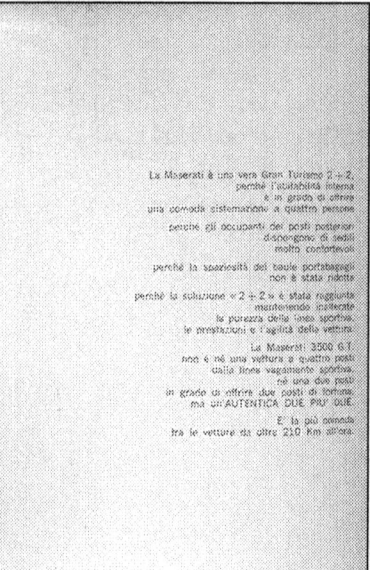

Page 6:
Background - white
Print - black

3500 GT - TIPO 101			section 7-16	141
3500 GT - 5000 - 7/61				
color folder	8³/₁₆ x 11½"	21 x 29.3 cm	ITA, FRA, ENG, DEU	Style 6

Page 7:
Background - black
Car interior - white leather, dark red car
Border & print - white

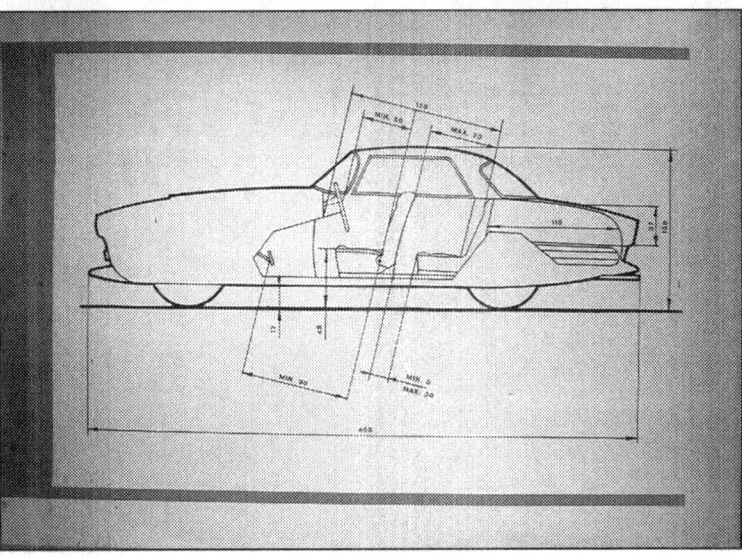

Page 8:
Background - white
Border - red
Car outline & dimensions - black

142	**3500 GT - TIPO 101**	section 7-16	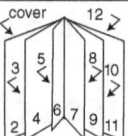
	3500 GT - 5000 - 7/61		
	color folder 8³/₁₆ x 11¹/₂" 21 x 29.3 cm ITA, FRA, ENG, DEU		Style 6

Page 9:
Color photo - dark blue car
Sky - blue
Earth - brown
Left stripe - black

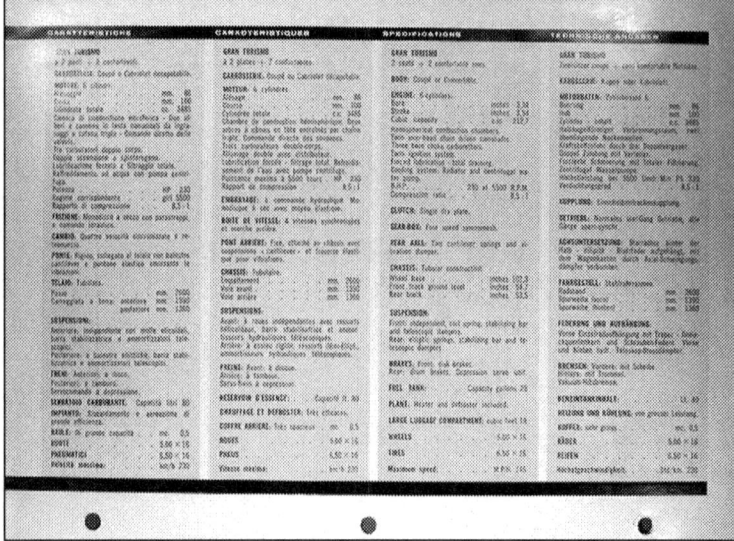

Page 10:
Background - white
Top stripe - black with white print
Bottom stripe - black
Background specifications - yellow
Print - black

3500 GT - TIPO 101			section 7-16		143
3500 GT - 5000 - 7/61					
color folder	8³/₁₆ x 11½"	21 x 29.3 cm	ITA, FRA, ENG, DEU	Style 6	

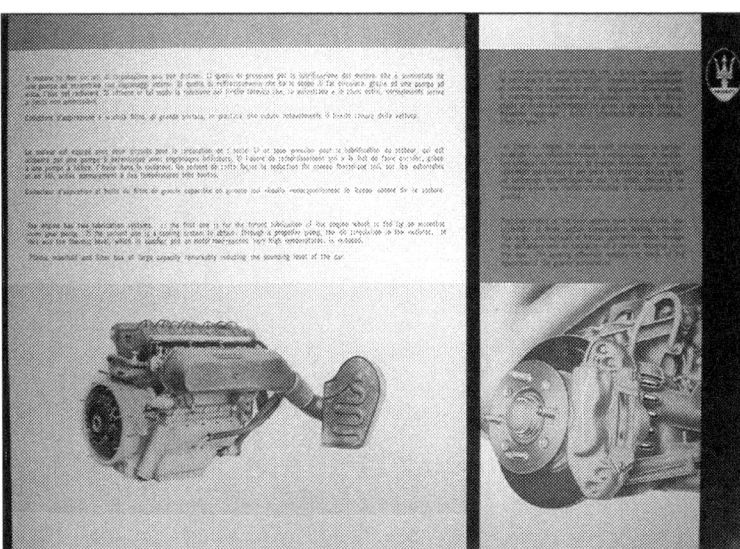

Page 11:
Background - white
Top left square: red
    vertical lines - white
    remainder - black
Right top square - red
    print - black
Engine - black and white photo tinted yellow
Suspension - black and white photo
Maserati badge - white on black band
Print - black

Page 12:
Background - white
Cars: left - red
    right - yellow with red interior
Left rectangle - red
Maserati badge - red on grey background
Print - black

Marked:
5000 - 7/61 Officine Grafiche Calderini - Bologna Studio Calderini

3500 GT - TIPO 101

3500 GT A CARBURATORI
3500 GT A INIEZIONE

| black and white sheet | 12 x 8¼" | 30.4 x 21 cm | ITA, FRA, ENG, DEU | Style 2B |

section 7-17

Front:
Background - white
Print - black
Cars - black and white photos

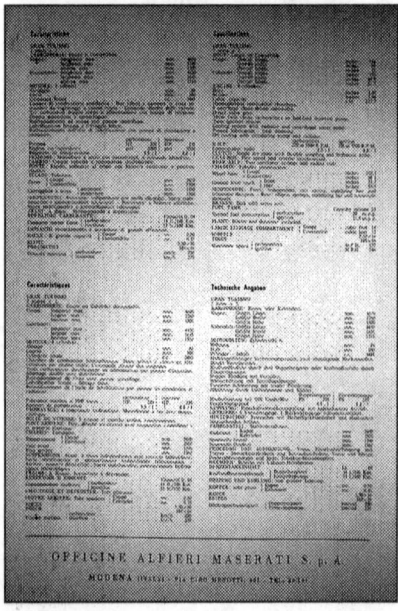

Rear:
Background - white
Print - black

Marked:
None

3500 GT - TIPO 101

3500 GT A CARBURATORI
3500 GT A INIEZIONE

| black and white sheet | 11⁵/₈ x 8¹/₄" | 29.6 x 21 cm | ITA, FRA, ENG, DEU | Style 2B |

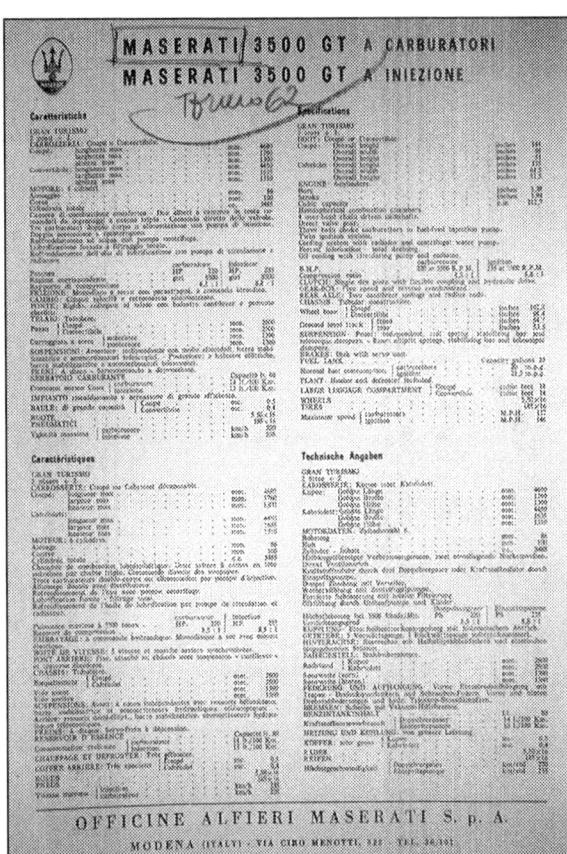

Front:
Background - white
Print - black

Marked:
Torino 62

Rear:
Blank

Marked:
None

3500 GT - TIPO 101　　section 7-19

3500 G.T. - A CARBURATORI - A INIEZIONE

| black and white brochure | 8¹/₁₆ x 12³/₁₆" | 20.6 x 31 cm | ITA, FRA, ENG, DEU | Style 3 |

Cover:
Black and white illustration
Maserati badge - blue and red on white

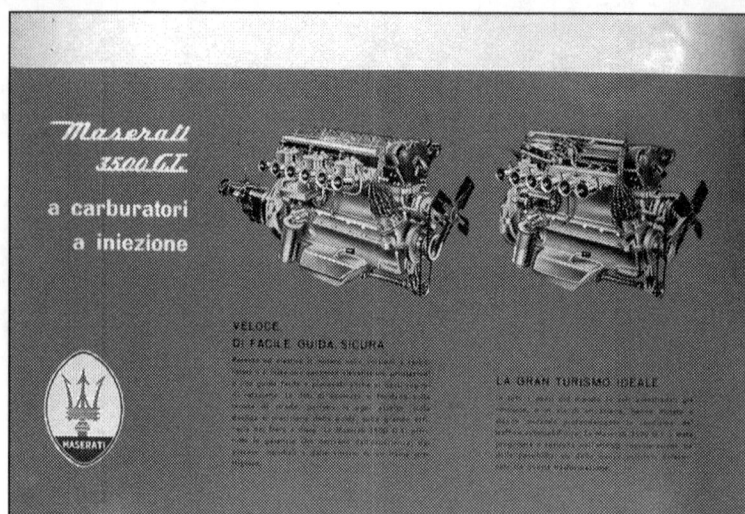

Page 2:
Background - red
Top band - white
Maserati badge - blue and red on white
Motors - black and white photos
Headings upper left - white
Print - black

3500 GT - TIPO 101	section 7-19

3500 G.T. - A CARBURATORI - A INIEZIONE

| black and white brochure | 8¹/₁₆ x 12³/₁₆" | 20.6 x 31 cm | ITA, FRA, ENG, DEU | Style 3 |

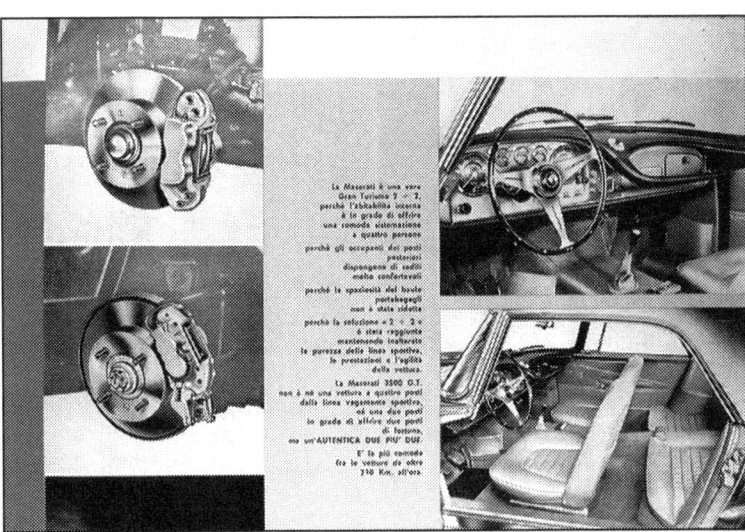

Page 3:
Background - white
Photos - black and white
Left vertical band - red
Center vertical band - grey / green with black print
Lower left band - black

Page 4:
Background - white
Left/right vertical bands - red
Car - black and white photo
Print - black

148	3500 GT - TIPO 101			section 7-19	
	3500 G.T. - A CARBURATORI - A INIEZIONE				
	black and white brochure	8¹/₁₆ x 12³/₁₆"	20.6 x 31 cm	ITA, FRA, ENG, DEU	Style 3

Page 5:
Background - white
Left/right vertical bands - red
Car - black and white photo
Print - black

Page 6:
Background - white
Left/right vertical
   bands - blue
Car - black and white photo
Print - black

3500 GT - TIPO 101

3500 G.T. - A CARBURATORI - A INIEZIONE

section 7-19

| black and white brochure | 8¹/₁₆ x 12³/₁₆" | 20.6 x 31 cm | ITA, FRA, ENG, DEU | Style 3 |

Page 7:
Background - white
Left/right vertical band - blue
Car - black and white photo
Print - black

Page 8:
Background - white
Top headings - red
Bottom band - blue with white print
Vertical bands - grey / green
Print - black

Marked:
STAB. POL. ARTIOLI - MODENA - STUDIO KOKY

3500 GT - TIPO 101	section 7-20	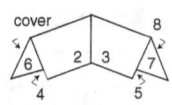

3500 G.T. CARBURATORI INIEZIONE (REPRINTED)

| 1, 2 b&w brochure original | 8 x 12¼" | 20.5 x 31 cm | ITA, FRA, ENG, DEU | Style 3 |
| 3 b&w brochure reprint | 8 x 12¼" | 20.5 x 31 cm | | |

Cover:
Black and white illustration
Maserati badge - blue and
red on white

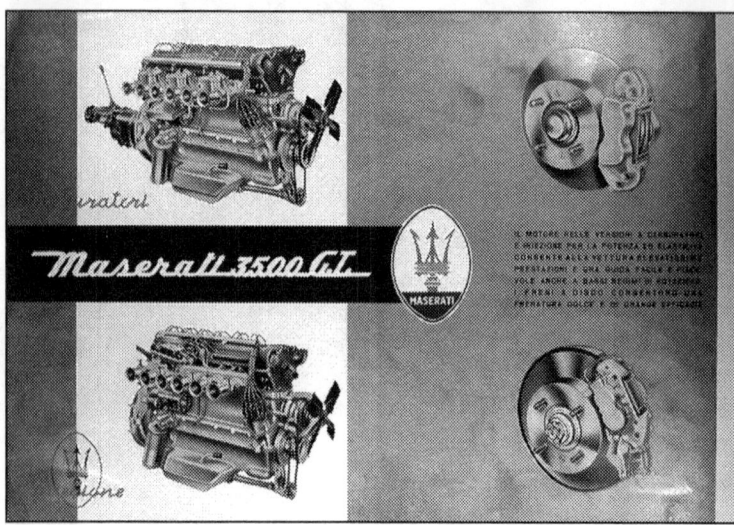

Page 2:
Background - white
Left/right bands - gold
Engines - black and
    white photos
Brakes - black and
    white photos
Maserati badge - blue
    and red on white
Carburatori - red
Iniezione - red
Maserati 3500 G.T. - white
    on black band
Print - black

3500 GT - TIPO 101

3500 G.T. CARBURATORI INIEZIONE

section 7-20

| 1, 2 b&w brochure original | 8 x 12¼" | 20.5 x 31 cm | ITA, FRA, ENG, DEU | Style 3 |
| 3 b&w brochure reprint | 8 x 12¼" | 20.5 x 31 cm | | |

Page 3:
Background - white
Photos - black and white
Horizontal band - red
Print - black

Page 4:
Background - white
Left/right vertical bands - gold
Car - black and white photo
Print - black

3500 GT - TIPO 101

152   **3500 G.T. CARBURATORI INIEZIONE**

section 7-20   Style 3

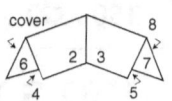

1, 2 b&w brochure original	8 x 12¼"	20.5 x 31 cm	ITA, FRA, ENG, DEU	
3 b&w brochure reprint	8 x 12¼"	20.5 x 31 cm		

Page 5:
Background - white
Left / Right Vertical
    Bands - gold
Car - black and white photo
Print - black

Page 6:
Background - white
Left / Right Vertical
    Bands - blue
Car - black and white photo
Print - black

3500 GT - TIPO 101

3500 G.T. CARBURATORI INIEZIONE

section 7-20 | 153

| 1, 2 b&w brochure original | 8 x 12¼" | 20.5 x 31 cm | ITA, FRA, ENG, DEU | Style 3 |
| 3 b&w brochure reprint | 8 x 12¼" | 20.5 x 31 cm | | |

Page 7:
Background - white
Left/right vertical bands - blue
Car - black and white photo
Print - black

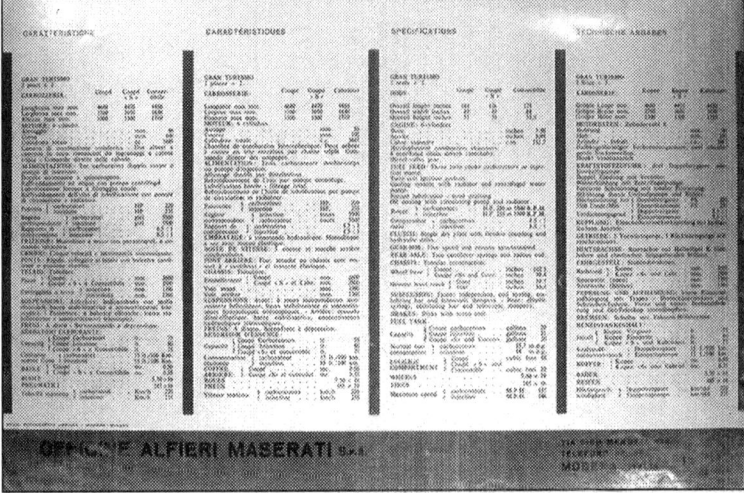

Page 8:
Background - white
Top headings - red
Bands - gold
Print: black

Marked
1. STAB. POLIGRAFICO ARTIOLI - MODENA - MILANO
2. STABILIMENTO POLIGRAFICO ARTIOLI - MODENA
3. Reprint marked STABILIMENTO POLIGRAFICO ARTIOLI - MODENA Gold is more a brown, rear bottom band 3/4" (2.3 cm) high <u>NOT MARKED</u> 1998 Archivo Maserati riproduzione anastatica

3500 GT - TIPO 101			section 7-21	
154	**VETTURA MASERATI 3500 GT A CARBURATORI**			
black and white card	5¹³/₁₆ x 8¹/₄"	14.8 x 21 cm	Italian	Style 2A

Front:
Background - white
Print - black

Rear:
Background - white
Blank

Marked:
None

3500 GT - TIPO 101

3500 GT A INIEZIONE

| black and white card | 5¹³/₁₆ x 8¹/₄" | 14.8 x 21 cm | Italian | Style 2A |

section 7-22

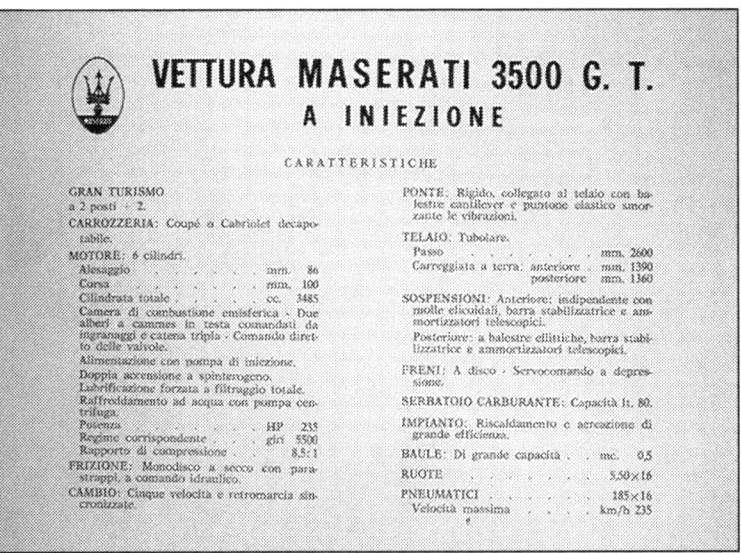

Front:
Background - white
Print - black

Rear:
Background - white
Blank

Marked:
None

Sometimes the card came with photograph as shown below:

3500 GT - TIPO 101

section 7-23

3500 G.T. WITH CARBURETTORS

| black and white sheet | 10 x 8" | 25.5 x 20.4 cm | English | Style 2B |

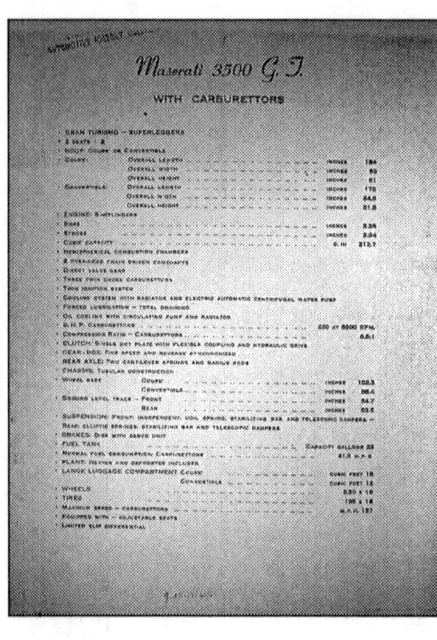

Front:
Background - white
Print - black

Rear:
Background - white
Blank

Marked:
None

3500 GT - TIPO 101

MASERATI 3500 G.T. FUEL INJECTION

section 7-24

157

| black and white sheet | 10 x 8" | 25.5 x 20.4 cm | English | Style 2B |

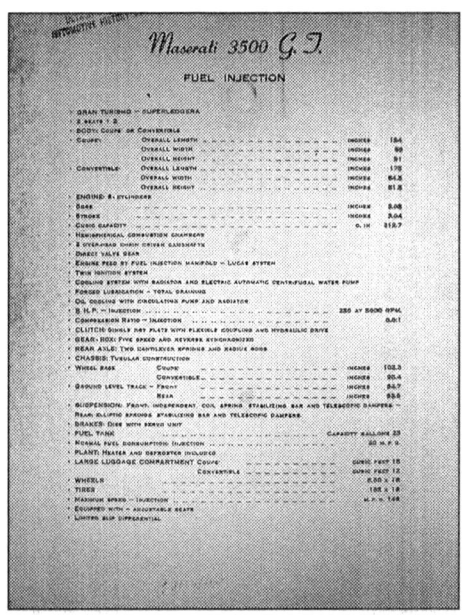

Front:
Background - white
Print - black

Rear:
Background - white
Blank

Marked:
None

158	**3500 GT - TIPO 101**	section 7-25	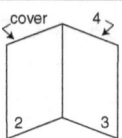

3500 GT SPYDER

| color brochure | 8¼ x 11¹³⁄₁₆" | 21 x 29.7 cm | ITA, FRA, ENG, DEU | Style 1 |

Cover:
Background - white
Color photo - silver car, red interior

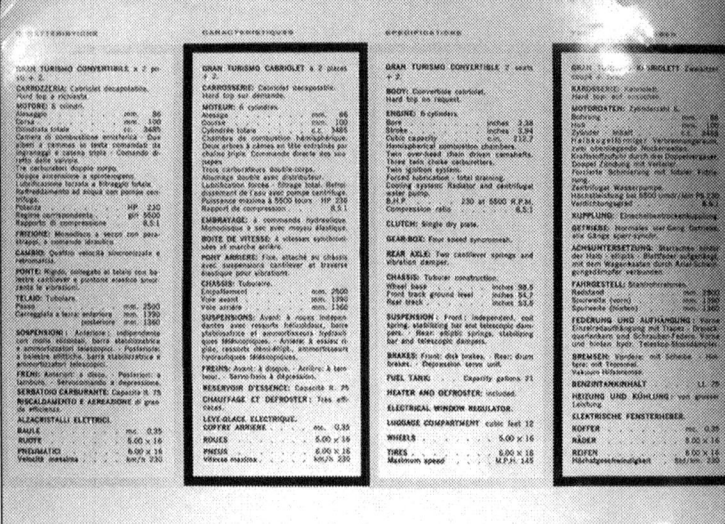

Page 2:
Background - white
Top headings - blue
1 & 3 spec borders - yellow
2 & 4 spec borders - black
Print - black

3500 GT - TIPO 101			section 7-25		159
3500 GT SPYDER					
color brochure	8¼ x 11¹³/₁₆"	21 x 29.7 cm	ITA, FRA, ENG, DEU	Style 1	

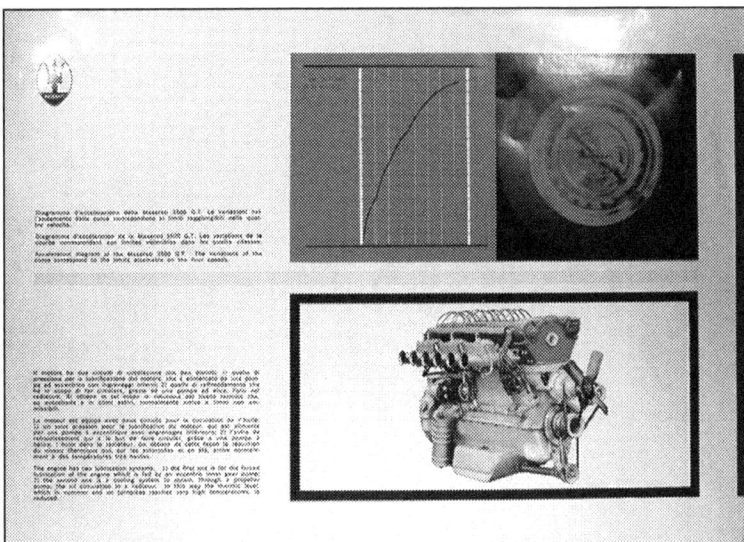

Page 3:
Background - white
Maserati badge - black
Engine - black and white
    photo with black border
Wheel - black and white
    photo tinted red
Graph background - red
Graph vertical lines - white
Graph horizontal lines and
    print - black
Print - black

Page 4:
Color photo:
    top down car - yellow
    with black interior
    top up car - black with
    red interior
Top border - light purple
Bottom border - white
Maserati badge - red
Manelli e rondelli - blue
Print - black

Marked:
Studio Calderini - Officine Grafiche Calderini - Bologna
Manelli e Rondelli

160	**3500 GT - TIPO 101**	section 7-26	
	3500 GT SPYDER 1961		
	black and white sheet	8¼ x 11¾" — 21 x 29.9 cm — ITA, FRA, ENG, DEU	Style 2A

Front:
Background - white
Car - black and white photo
Print - black

Rear:
Background - white
Print - black

Marked:
Studio Calderini - Officine Grafiche Calderini - Bologna - 1961

3500 GT - TIPO 101			section 7-26		161
3500 GT SPYDER					
black and white sheet	8¼ x 11¾"	21 x 29.9 cm	ITA, FRA, ENG, DEU	Style 2A	

3500 Spyder Photos

162	**3500 GT - TIPO 101**	section 7-27	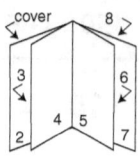
	3500 GT BERLINA ANNO 1960 OMOLOGATO SHEET		
	black and white sheet	11¹¹/₁₆ x 8¼" 29.6 x 21 cm Italian	Style 5

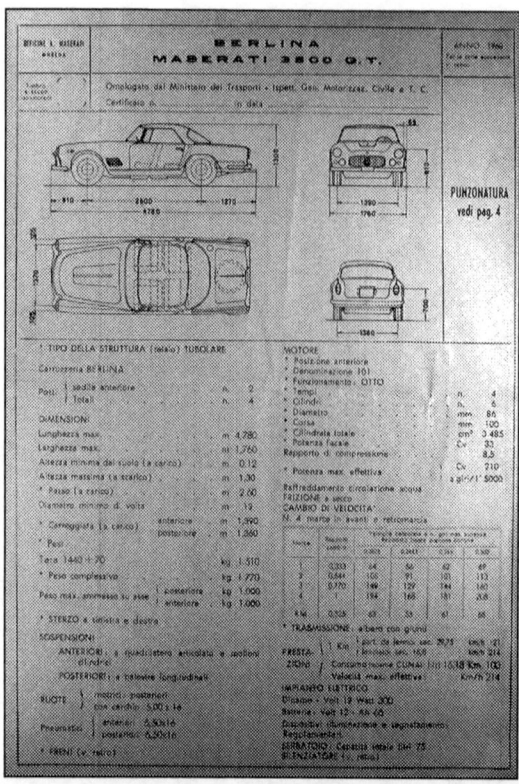

Cover:
Background - off white
Print - black

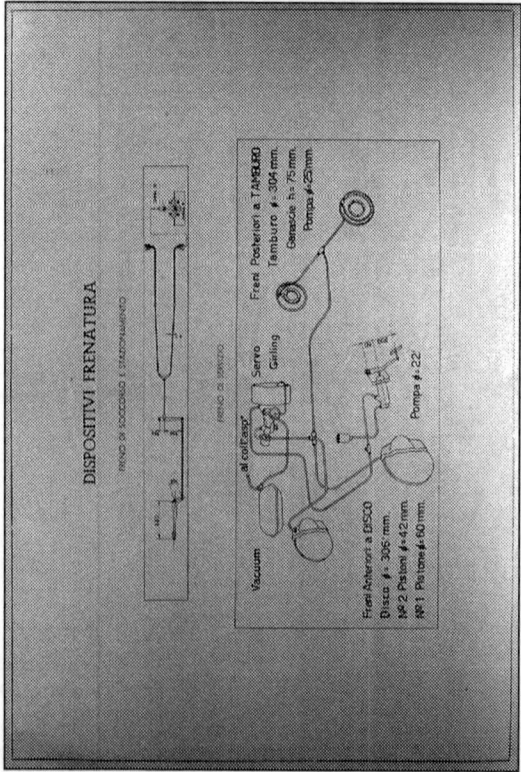

Page 2:
Background - off white
Print - black

NOTE: MANY OF THESE SHEETS WERE PREPARED AS CHANGES WERE MADE TO EACH MODEL. THIS IS JUST ONE EXAMPLE THAT CAN BE FOUND. ALL OF THE MODELS PRODUCED SHOULD HAVE SHEETS PREPARED.

3500 GT - TIPO 101		section 7-27		163
3500 GT BERLINA ANNO 1960 OMOLOGATO SHEET				
black and white sheet	11¹¹/₁₆ x 8¼"	29.6 x 21 cm	Italian	Style 5

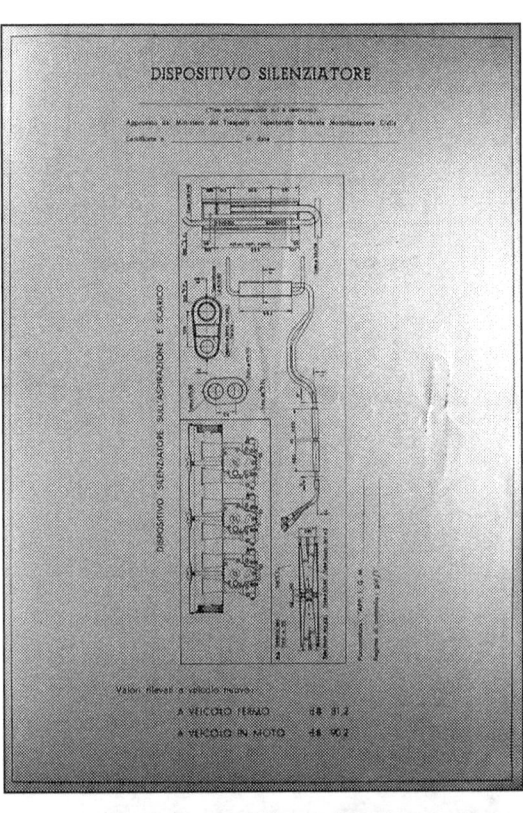

Page 3:
Background - off white
Print - black

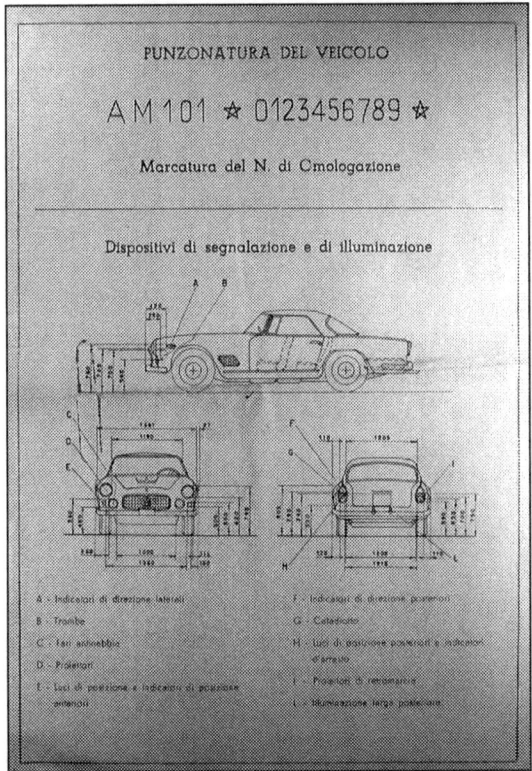

Page 4:
Background - off white
Print - black

Marked:
None

164	**3500 GT - TIPO 101**	section 7-28	
	TOWN & COUNTRY REPRINT		
	black and white folder	11⁵/₈ x 9¹¹/₁₆" 32 x 24.5 cm	English	Style 1

Cover:

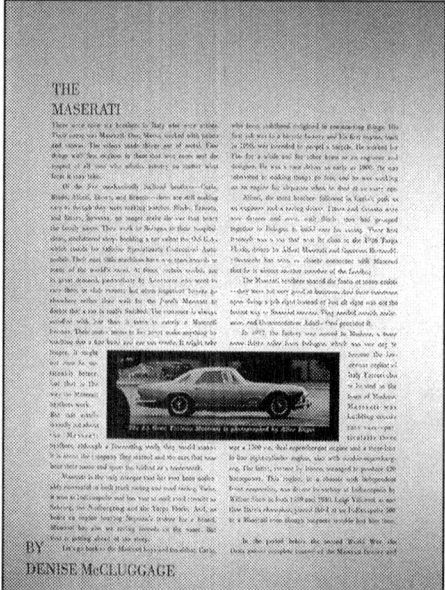

Page 2:

Page 3:

Page 4:

All pages:
Background - white
Print - black

SEBRING 1963-1970 (TIPO AM101)

8.0

SEBRING 2+2 (SERIES II) 3500	8-1
SEBRING 2+2 3500	8-2
SEBRING 3500, 3700, 4000 cc	8-3
SEBRING 3500, 3700, 4000 cc	8-4

Sebring 1963-1970 (TIPO AM101)		section 8-1		
166	**SEBRING 2+2 (SERIES II) 3500**			
	black and white sheet	12 x 8⁵/₁₆" / 30.5 x 21.2 cm	ITA, FRA, DEU, ENG	Style 2B

Front:
Background - white
Cars - black and white photos

Rear:
Background - white
Print - black

Marked:
None

Sebring 1963-1970 (TIPO AM101)	section 8-2		167

SEBRING 2+2 3500

| black and white brochure | 7¹/₁₆ x 9¹¹/₁₆" | 18 x 24.7 cm | ITA, ENG, DEU, FRA | Style 1 |

Two identical brochures - Page four specification language is the only difference

Cover:
Background:
Left half - black with white print
Right half - red with black print

Page 2:
Background - white
Car - black and white photo
Print - black

| 168 | Sebring 1963-1970 (TIPO AM101) | section 8-2 | 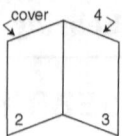 |

SEBRING 2+2 3500

| black and white brochure | 7¹/₁₆ x 9¹¹/₁₆" | 18 x 24.7 cm | ITA, ENG, DEU, FRA | Style 1 |

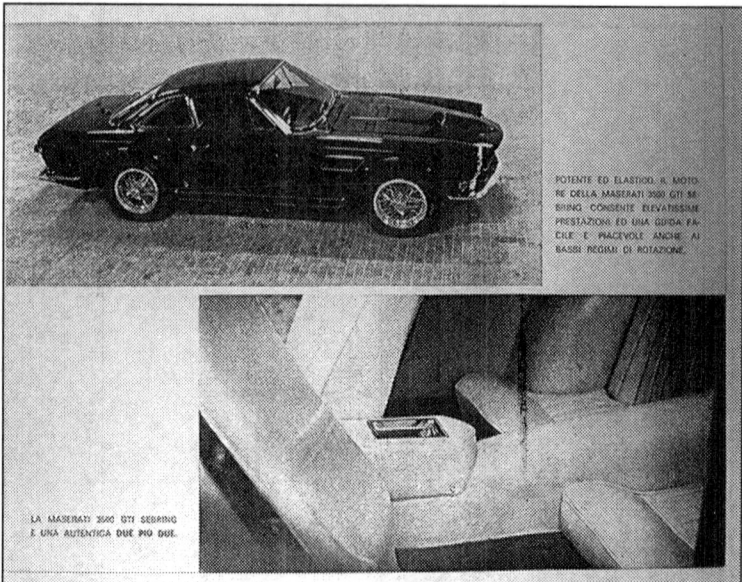

Page 3:
Background - white
Car - black and white photo
Interior - black and white photo
Print - black in Italian for both brochures

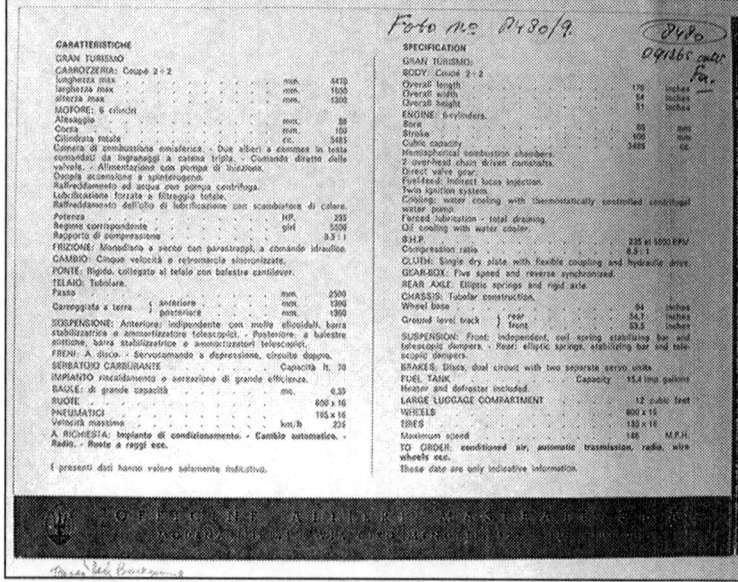

Page 4:
(one brochure in ITA, ENG and one brochure in DEU, FRA)
Background - white
Bottom border - red
All print - black

Marked:
None

Sebring 1963-1970 (TIPO AM101)		section 8-3	
SEBRING 3500, 3700, 4000 cc			
black and white brochure	6¹/₄ x 12⁵/₈" · 16 x 32.2 cm	ITA, ENG, DEU, FRA	Style 10

Cover:
Background - white
Maserati badge - blue and red
Maserati - red
Sebring - black
Car - black and white photo in black surround

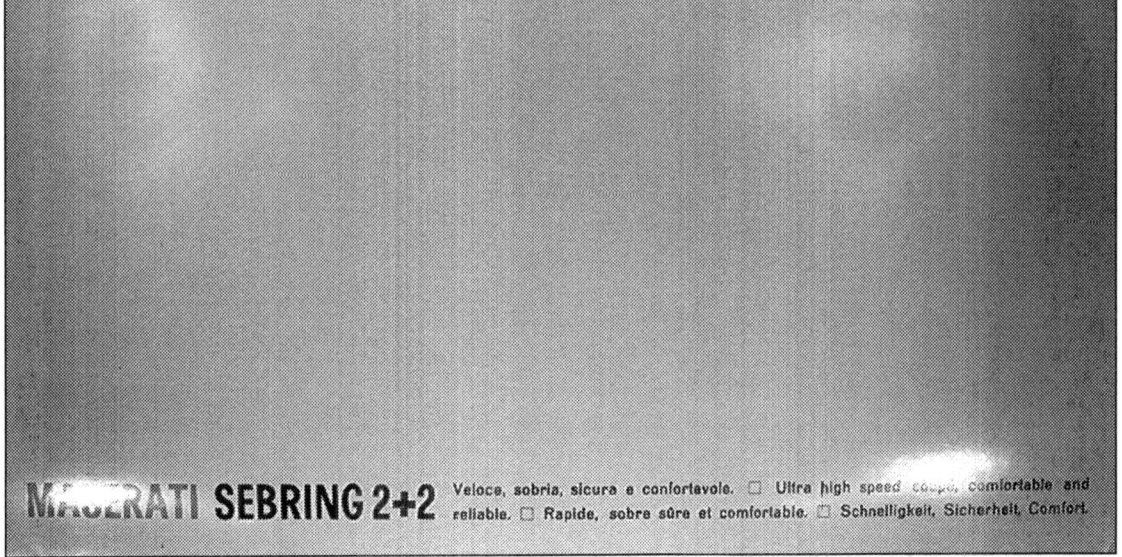

Page 2:
Background - white
Maserati - red
Print - black

170	Sebring 1963-1970 (TIPO AM101)	section 8-3	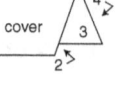
	SEBRING 3500, 3700, 4000 cc		
	black and white brochure · 6¼ x 12⅝" · 16 x 32.2 cm · ITA, ENG, DEU, FRA		Style 10

Page 3:
Car - black and white photo

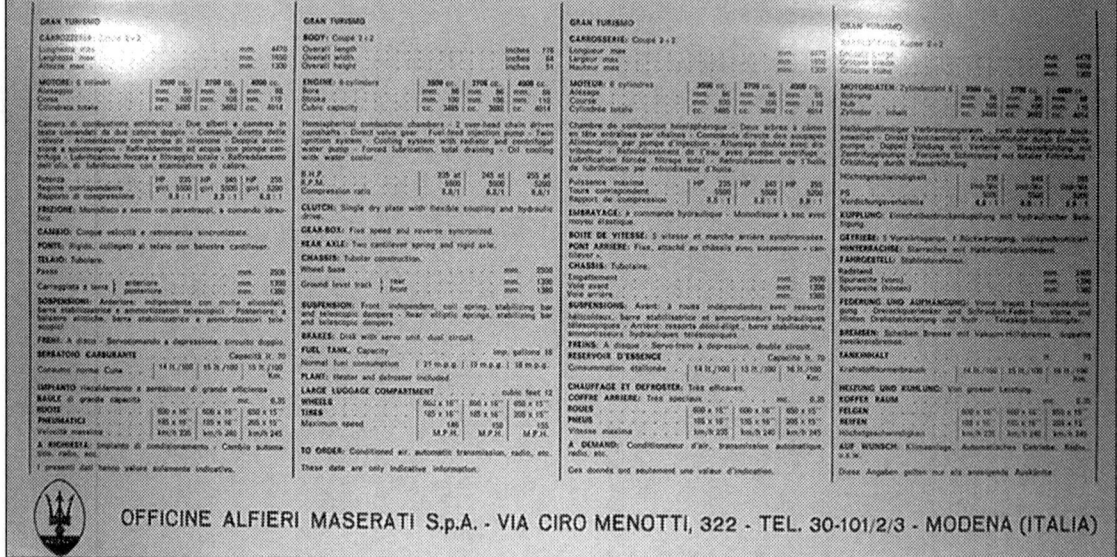

Page 4:
Background - white
Print - black

Marked:
None

Sebring 1963-1970 (TIPO AM101)	section 8-4		171
SEBRING 3500, 3700, 4000 cc			
color brochure	6¼ x 12⅝"	16 x 32 cm	ITA, FRA, ENG, DEU	Style 9

Cover:
Background - white
Maserati - red
Sebring - black
Cars - color photos, silver

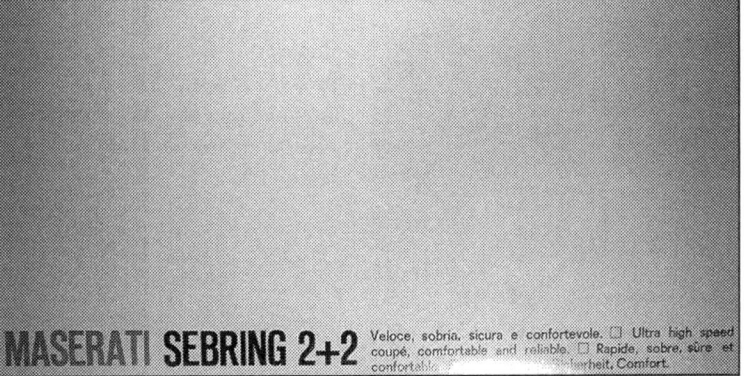

Page 2:
Background - white
Maserati - red
Print - black

Page 3:
Car - color photo, silver with black interior

172	Sebring 1963-1970 (TIPO AM101)		section 8-4	
	SEBRING 3500, 3700, 4000 cc			
	color brochure	6¼ x 12⅝"	16 x 32 cm	ITA, FRA, ENG, DEU	Style 9

Page 4:
Background - white
Car, front - color photo, silver
Car, rear - black and white photo
Line - black

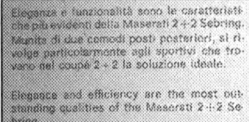 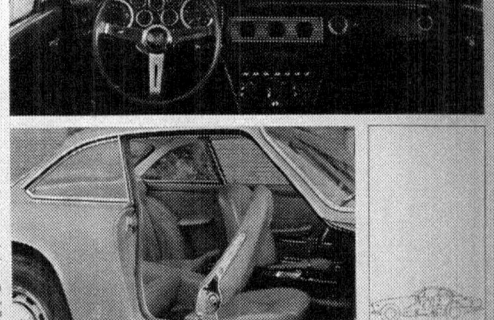

Page 5:
Background - white
Interior photos - color photos, silver car, brown interior
Print - black

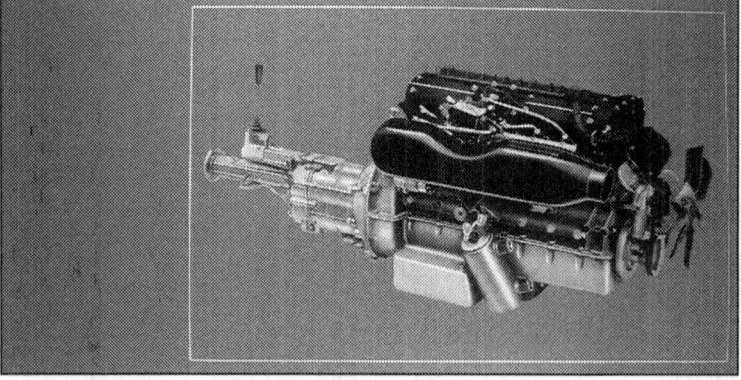

Page 6:
Background - red
Engine - black and white photo
Outline - white

Sebring 1963-1970 (TIPO AM101)	section 8-4	
SEBRING 3500, 3700, 4000 cc		173
color brochure	6¼ x 12⅝"	16 x 32 cm	ITA, FRA, ENG, DEU	Style 9

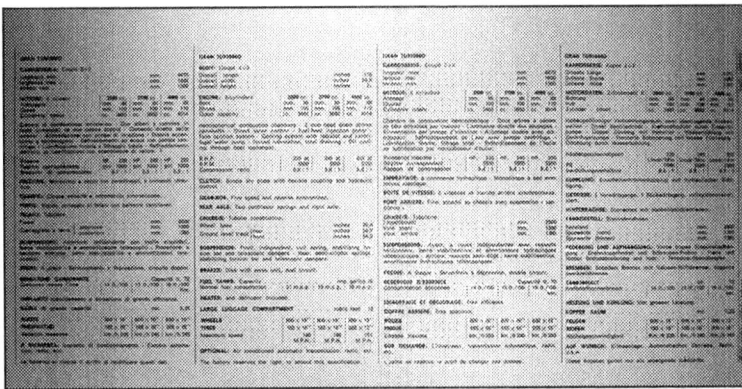

Page 7:
Background - white
Vertical lines - red
Print - black

Page 8:
Background - white
Maserati badge - blue and red
Print - black

Marked: (on page 7)
Officine Grafiche Colderini Bologna - Studio Calderini

MISTRAL 1964-1970 (TIPO AM109)

9.0

VETTURA BERLINA "2 POSTI" 3500	9-1
2 POSTI MISTRAL 3700	9-2
2 POSTI 3700	9-3
MISTRAL 3700, 4000	9-4
MISTRAL 3700, 4000	9-5
AUTOVETTURA TIPO AM 109 - 2 POSTI 3700	9-6
MASERATI PRICE LIST PRE 1968 USA SPECIFICATIONS	9-7

176	MISTRAL 1964-1970 (TIPO AM109)		section 9-1	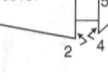
	VETTURA BERLINA "2 POSTI" 3500			
	2 folders & sheet	8¼ x 11¾" 21 x 29.8 cm	Italian	Style 13

Cover Folder

Cover:
Left border - red with white print
Body - dark blue
Maserati badge - blue and red
Produzione "1964" - silver

Pages 2, 3 & 4:
White - blank

Page 5:
Background - dark blue
Illustration - white

Page 6:
Background - dark blue
Maserati badge - blue and red on white
Print & line - white

MISTRAL 1964-1970 (TIPO AM109)			section 9-1		
VETTURA BERLINA "2 POSTI" 3500					177
2 folders & sheet	8¼ x 11¾"	21 x 29.8 cm	Italian	Style 1	

Inside Folder

Cover:
Background - white
Print - black

Pages 2, 3, 4:
Background - white
Blank

Sheet Front:
Style 2A
Background - white
Print - black

Rear:
Background - white
Blank

Marked:
None

Other black and white photos were probably included

178	MISTRAL 1964-1970 (TIPO AM109)		section 9-2	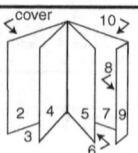
	2 POSTI MISTRAL 3700			
	1 color brochure original 2 color brochure reprint	8¼ x 11¹³⁄₁₆" 8¼ x 12"	21 x 29.8 cm 21 x 30.4 cm	ITA, FRA, DEU, ENG	Style 8

Cover:
Background:
    Left - grey
    Right - black
2 POSTI - white
Mistral - red

Page 2:
Background - white
Photo - black and white
MASERATI - red
DUE POSTI - black
Car - white

MISTRAL 1964-1970 (TIPO AM109)			section 9-2		179
2 POSTI MISTRAL 3700					
1 color brochure original 2 color brochure reprint	8¼ x 11¹³/₁₆" 8¼ x 12"	21 x 29.8 cm 21 x 30.4 cm	ITA, FRA, DEU, ENG	Style 8	

Page 3:
Color photo: coupe, white
spyder, red with tan interior

Page 4:
Background - white
Car, side view - red with tan interior
Car, front and rear - black and white photo
Print and border - black

MISTRAL 1964-1970 (TIPO AM109)		section 9-2	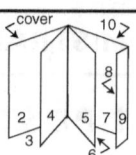
180	**2 POSTI MISTRAL 3700**		
1 color brochure original	8¼ x 11¹³⁄₁₆"	21 x 29.8 cm	ITA, FRA, DEU, ENG	Style 8
2 color brochure reprint	8¼ x 12"	21 x 30.4 cm		

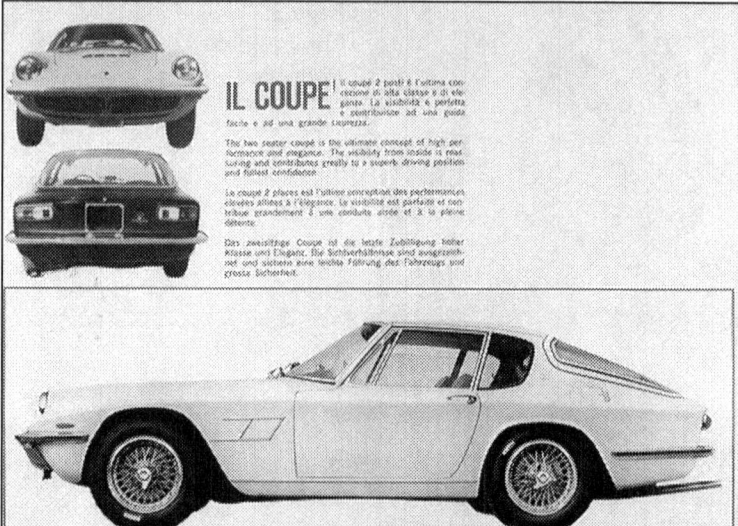

Page 5:
Background - white
Car, side view - white
Car, front & rear - black and white photo
Print and border - black

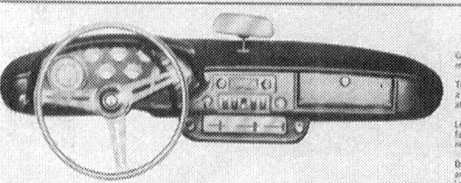

Page 6:
Background - white
Interior - color photo, red car with tan interior
Instrument panel - black and white photo
Print and border - black

MISTRAL 1964-1970 (TIPO AM109)

2 POSTI MISTRAL 3700

| 1 color brochure original | 8¼ x 11¹³/₁₆" | 21 x 29.8 cm | ITA, FRA, DEU, ENG | Style 8 |
| 2 color brochure reprint | 8¼ x 12" | 21 x 30.4 cm | | |

section 9-2

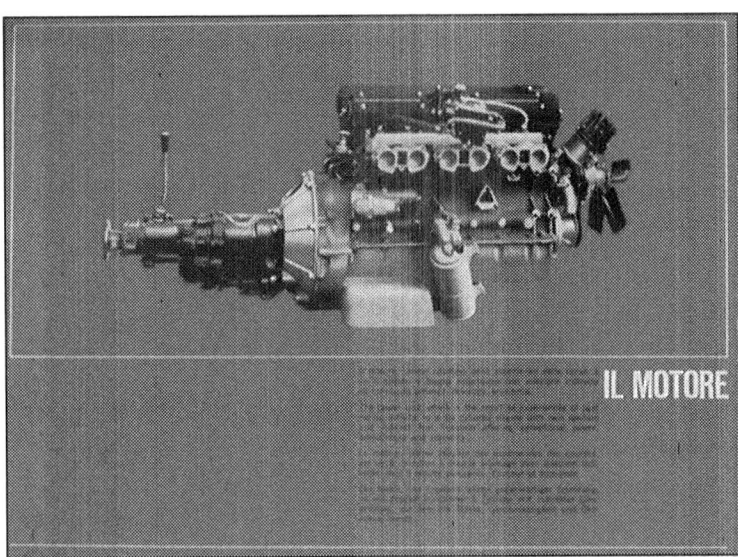

Page 7:
Background - red
Engine - black and white photo
IL MOTORE - white
Border and line - white
Print - black

Page 8:
Background - white
Border - red
Maserati - black
DUE POSTI - red
Italian - black
English - red
French - black
German - red

182	MISTRAL 1964-1970 (TIPO AM109)		section 9-2	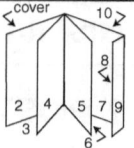	
	2 POSTI MISTRAL 3700				
	1 color brochure original 2 color brochure reprint	8¼ x 11¹³⁄₁₆" 8¼ x 12"	21 x 29.8 cm 21 x 30.4 cm	ITA, FRA, DEU, ENG	Style 8

Page 9:
Background - red
Print - black

Page 10:
Background - white
MASERATI - red
Border - red
Maserati badge - red
Print - black

Marked:
1. Officine Grafiche Calderini - via Emilia Levante, 312 - Bologna Studio Calderini Manelli e Rondelli 8¼ x 11¹³⁄₁₆"

2. Reprint NOT MARKED 1998 Archivio Maserati riproduzione anastatica Maserati Badge bottom part cut off. Reprint darker red than original bright red. Reprint shows 'aging' on back of each end.
8¼ x 12"

MISTRAL 1964-1970 (TIPO AM109)

section 9-3

2 POSTI 3700

183

| black and white sheet | 7 ⁷/₈ x 11 ⁹/₁₆" | 20 x 29.5 cm | ITA, FRA, DEU, ENG | Style 2A |

Front:
Background - grey
Print - black

Rear:
Background - grey
Blank

Can be found in Brochure 9-1.

Marked:
None

184	MISTRAL 1964-1970 (TIPO AM109)	section 9-4	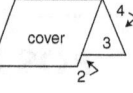
	MISTRAL 3700, 4000		
	black and white folder · 6 ¼ x 12 ⅝" · 16 x 32 cm · ITA, FRA, DEU, ENG		Style 10

Cover:
Background - white
Maserati badge - red
Maserati - red
Mistral - black
Cars - black and white photos
surrounded by black rectangles

Page 2:
Background - white
Maserati - red
Print - black

Page 3:
Cars - black and white photo

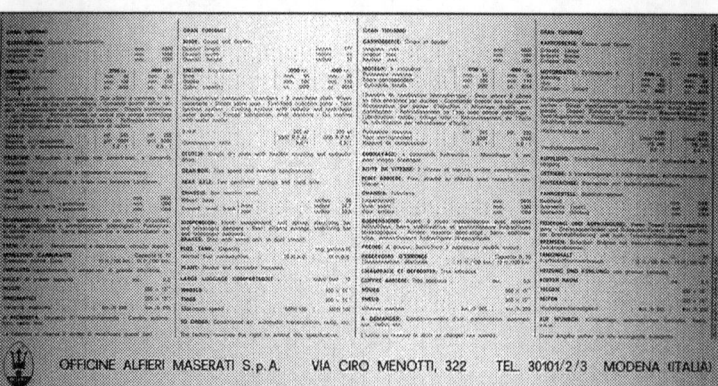

Page 4:
Background - white
Print - black

Marked:
Officine Grafiche Calderini
Bologna - Manelli e Rondelli

MISTRAL 1964-1970 (TIPO AM109)			section 9-5	
MISTRAL 3700, 4000				185
color brochure	6 ¼ x 12 ⁹⁄₁₆"	16 x 32 cm	ITA, FRA, DEU, ENG	Style 11

Cover:
Background - white
Maserati - red
Mistral - black
Cars - silver coupe, red spyder in black rectangle

Page 2:
Background - white
Maserati - red
Print - black

Page 3:
Color photo -
silver coupe -
black interior
gold spyder -
red interior

Page 4:
Background - white
Car - side view - silver car with black interior - red border
Car - front and rear - black and white photos
Print - black

186	MISTRAL 1964-1970 (TIPO AM109)	section 9-5	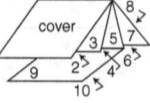	
	MISTRAL 3700, 4000			
	color brochure	6 ¹/₄ x 12 ⁹/₁₆"	16 x 32 cm	ITA, FRA, DEU, ENG	Style 11

Page 5:
Background - white
Color photos - silver car - tan interior with dark brown carpet
Print - black

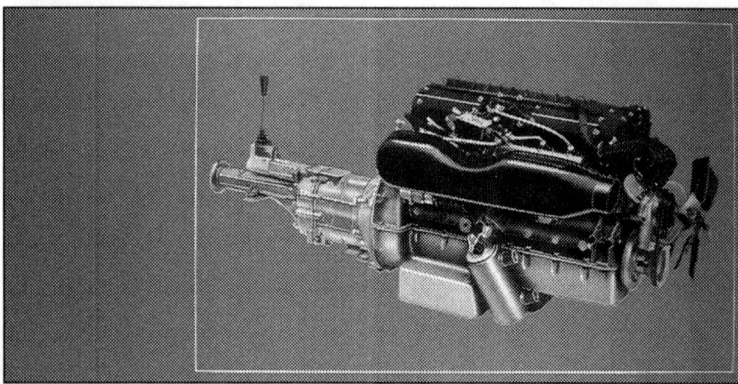

Page 6:
Background - red
Engine - black and white photo with white rectangle

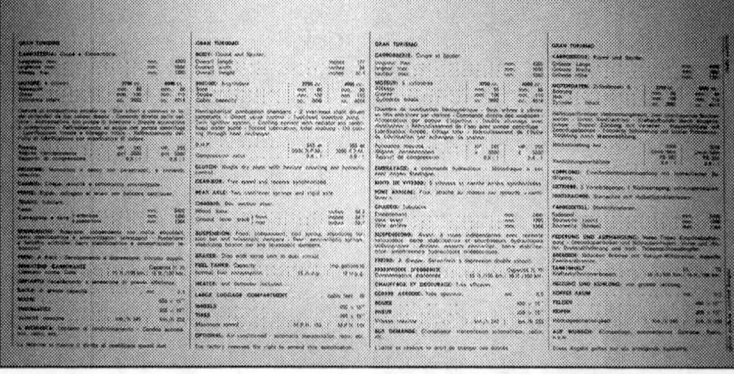

Page 7:
Background: - white
Vertical lines - red
Print - black

Page 8:
Background - white
Maserati badge: - blue and red
Print - black

MISTRAL 1964-1970 (TIPO AM109)		section 9-5	
MISTRAL 3700, 4000			
color brochure	6 ¼ x 12 ⁹⁄₁₆"	16 x 32 cm	ITA, FRA, DEU, ENG	Style 11

Page 9:
Background - white
Instrument panel - color photo - white interior
Print and illustration - black

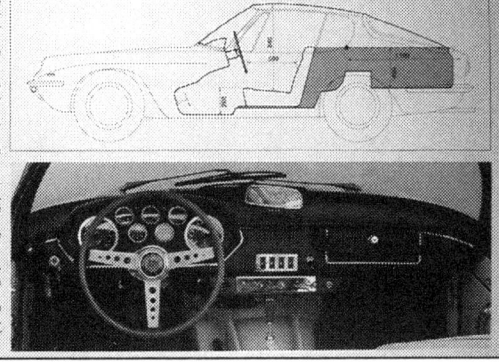

Page 10:
Background - white
Car - top down, red with tan interior - black border
Cars - black and white photos
Lower line - black

Marked (Page 7):
Officine Grafiche Calderini Bologna Studio Calderini

188	**MISTRAL 1964-1970 (TIPO AM109)**	section 9-6	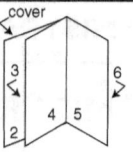
	AUTO VETTURA TIPO AM 109 - 2 POSTI		
	black and white folder	12¹/₁₆ x 8⁵/₈"	31 x 22 cm	Italian	Style 14

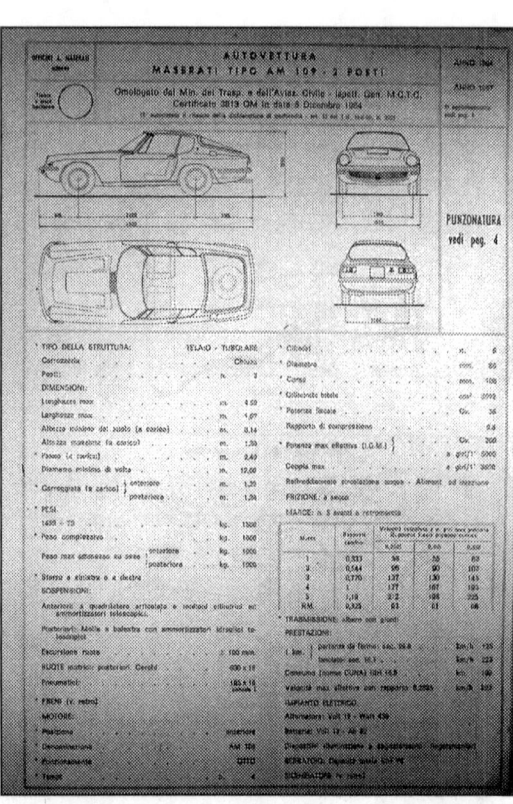

Cover:
Background - white
Print - black

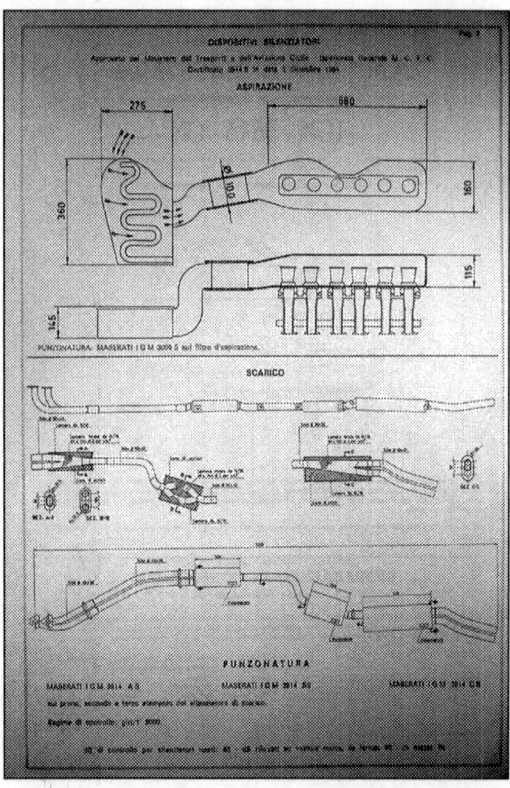

Page 2:
Background - white
Print - black

MISTRAL 1964-1970 (TIPO AM109)		section 9-6	
AUTO VETTURA TIPO AM 109 - 2 POSTI			
black and white folder	12¹/₁₆ x 8⁵/₈" / 31 x 22 cm	Italian	Style 14

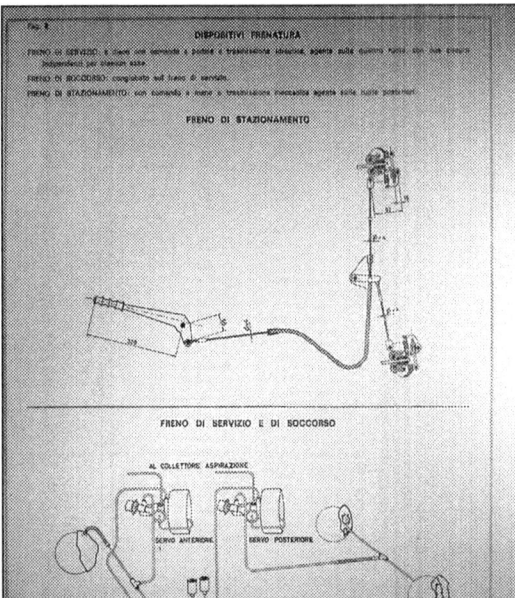

Page 3:
Background - white
Print - black

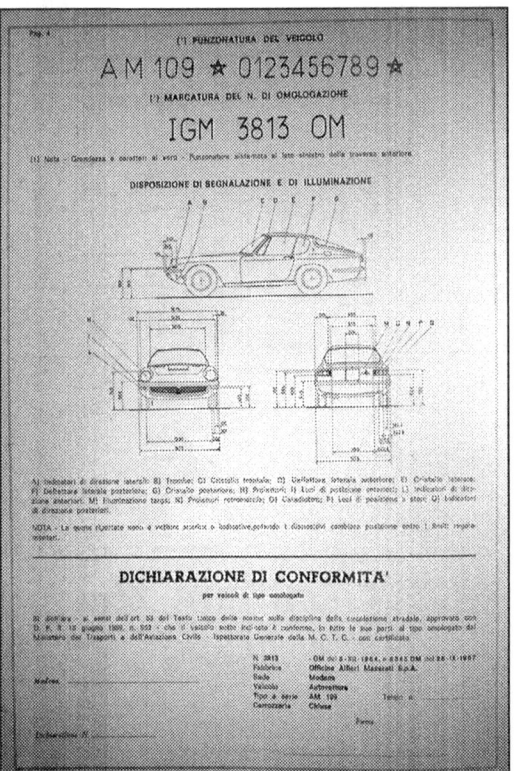

Page 4:
Background - white
Print - black

MISTRAL 1964-1970 (TIPO AM109)	section 9-6	
AUTO VETTURA TIPO AM 109 - 2 POSTI		Style 14
black and white folder	12¹/₁₆ x 8 ⁵/₈"	31 x 22 cm	Italian	

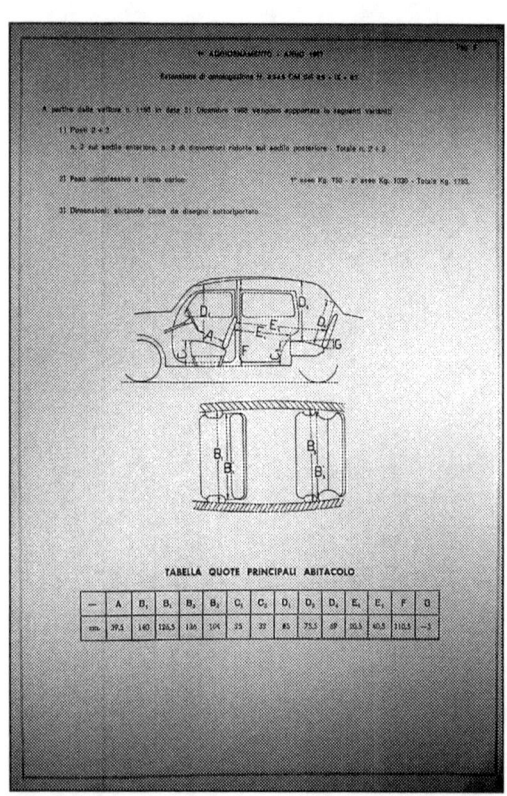

Page 5:
Background - white
Print - black

Page 6:
Background - white
Blank

Marked:
None

MISTRAL 1964-1970 (TIPO AM109)

MASERATI PRICE LIST - PRE 1968 USA SPECIFICATIONS

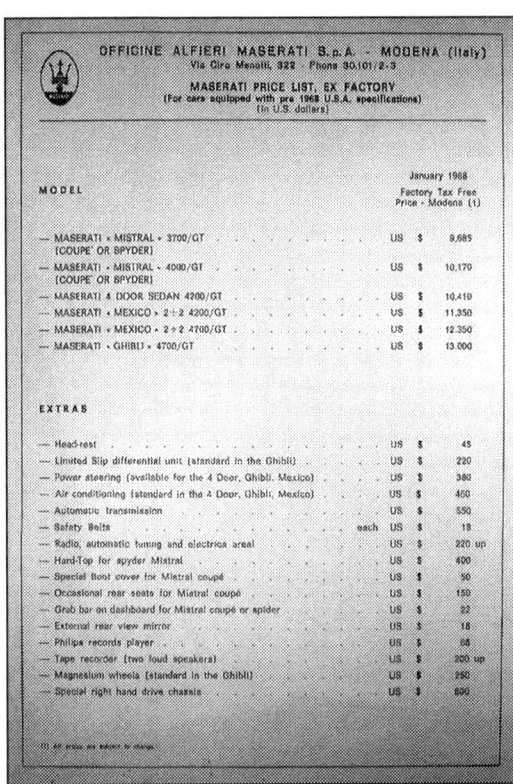

Front:
Background - white
Print - black

Rear:
Background - white
Blank

FULL LINE BROCHURES

MISTRAL, SEBRING, MEXICO, QUATTROPORTE, GHIBLI	10-1
MISTRAL, SEBRING, MEXICO, QUATTROPORTE, GHIBLI	10-2
4 PORTE, 2+2 SEBRING, 2 POSTI MISTRAL 1965	10-3
PRODUZIONE MASERATI 1966	10-4
PRODUZIONE MASERATI 1967	10-5

Full Line Brochures			section 10-1	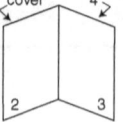
194 MISTRAL, SEBRING, MEXICO, QUATTROPORTE, GHIBLI				
black and white folder	11⁹/₁₆ x 9"	29.4 x 22.9 cm	Italian, English	Style 1

Cover:
Background - white
Maserati badge - blue and red
Car - black and white photo
Print - black

Page 2:
Background - white
Photos - black and white
Print - black

Full Line Brochures

MISTRAL, SEBRING, MEXICO, QUATTROPORTE, GHIBLI

| black and white folder | 11⁹/₁₆ x 9" | 29.4 x 22.9 cm | Italian, English | Style 1 |

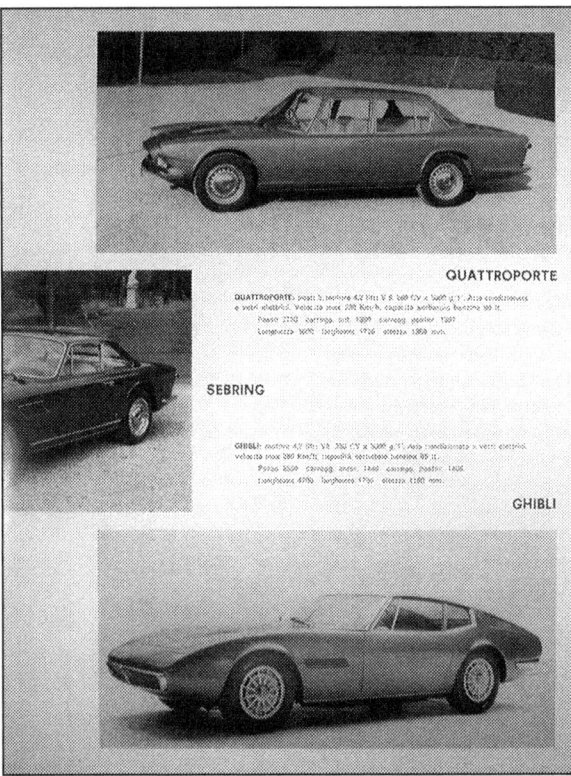

Page 3:
Background - white
Photos - black and white
Print - black
(quattroporte picture is different in 10-2)

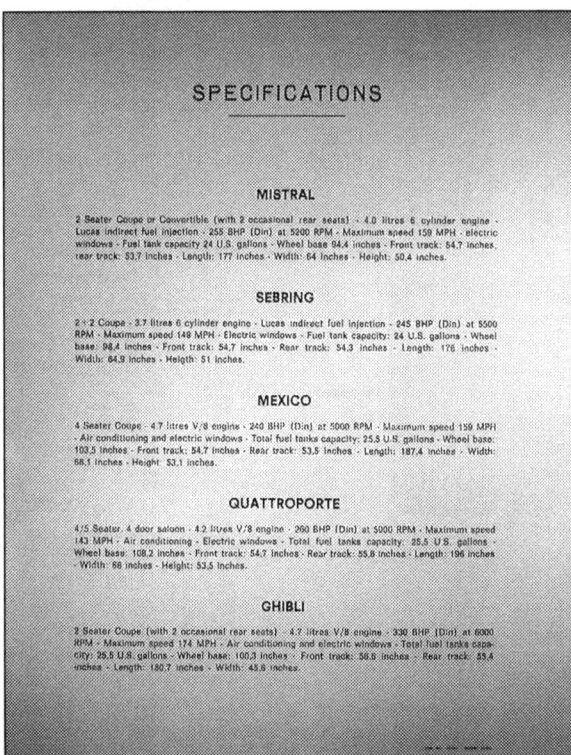

Page 4:
Background - white
Print - black

Marked:
STAB. POL. ARTIOLI - MODENA - MILANO

Full Line Brochures	section 10-2	
196 MISTRAL, SEBRING, MEXICO, QUATTROPORTE, GHIBLI		
black and white folder	11⁹/₁₆ x 9"	29.4 x 22.9 cm	Italian, English	Style 1

Cover:
Background - white
Maserati badge - blue and red
Car - black and white photo
Print - black

Page 2:
Background - white
Photos - black and white
Print - black

Full Line Brochures

MISTRAL, SEBRING, MEXICO, QUATTROPORTE, GHIBLI

| black and white folder | 11⁹/₁₆ x 9" | 29.4 x 22.9 cm | Italian, English | Style 1 |

section 10-2

Page 3:
Background - white
Photos - black and white
Print - black
(quattroporte picture is different in 10-1)

Page 4:
Background - white
Print - black

Marked:
STAB. POL. ARTIOLI - MODENA - MILANO

Full Line Brochures	section 10-3
198 — 4 PORTE, 2+2 SEBRING, 2 POSTI MISTRAL 1965	
black and white sheet — 11⁵/₈ x 8¼" — 29.6 x 21 cm — Italian	Style 2B

Front:
Background - white
Maserati badge - blue and red
Two lines - red
Print - black

Back:
Background - white
Blank

Marked:
None

Full Line Brochures

PRODUZIONE MASERATI 1966

| colored sheet | 11¹¹/₁₆ x 8³/₁₆" | 29.7 x 20.8 cm | Italian | Style 2B |

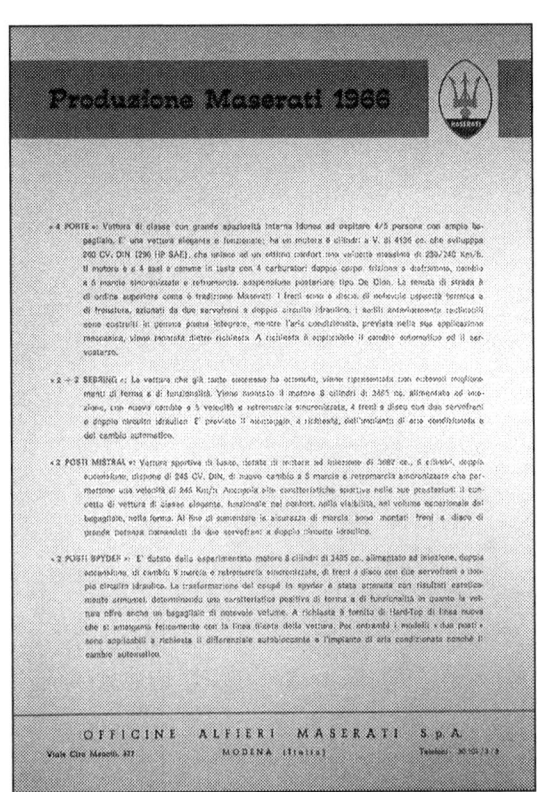

Front:
Background - grey/green
Maserati badge - blue and red
Top border - red
Car headings - red
Bottom line - red
Print - black

Rear:
Background - grey/green
Blank

Marked:
None

Full Line Brochures			section 10-5	
PRODUZIONE "MASERATI" 1967				
sheet	12³/₈ x 6³/₁₆"	31.5 x 15.8 cm	Italian	Style 2B

Front:
Background - white
Maserati badge - blue and red
Top heading - red
Car headings - red
Print - black

Rear:
Background - white
Blank

Marked:
None

BROCHURE LITERATURE FOLDERS   11.0

BROCHURE LITERATURE FOLDERS 1967   11-1
TO HOLD BROCHURES 10-5, 9-5, 8-4

BROCHURE LITERATURE FOLDER   11-2
USED TO HOLD VARIOUS PRESS RELEASES AND
SINGLE SHEETS SUCH AS
6-15, 6-16, 6-17, 6-18, 7-1 TO 7-9

Brochure Literature Folders		section 11-1	

BROCHURE LITERATURE FOLDERS 1967

folder	12⁷/₈ x 6⁹/₁₆"	32.5 x 16.6 cm	none	Style 15

Cover
Background - cream
Maserati badge - blue and red
Print - blue

Page 2,3
Background - white
Blank

Page 4,5
Background - cream
Blank

Enclosures
Brochures 10-5, 9-5, 8-4

Also Ghibli, Mexico and Quattroporte (not covered here)

Marked:
None

Brochure Literature Folders	section 11-2		
BROCHURE LITERATURE FOLDER		cover 1	
brochure holder	8¼ x 11¾"	21 x 30 cm	none	Style 7

Used to hold various press releases and single sheets such as 6-15, 6-16, 6-17, 6-18, 7-1 to 7-9

Front
Background - white
Maserati badge - red
MASERATI - black
Square and line - red

Pages 2, 3, 4
Background - white
Blank

Marked:
None

MOTOCICLI-CICLOMOTORI

TIPO 50/T2	12-1
L.125/T2, T.V. 125/T2, L.160/T4, 175/S4, 250/T4	12-2
TIPO 250/T4	12-3
LA TIPO 160/T4, LA TIPO 125/T2	12-4
MOTO CICLOMOTORI PRODUZIONE 1957	12-5
MOTOCICLI-CICLOMOTORI PRODUZIONE 1958 (REPRINTED)	12-6
CANDELE ACCUMULATORI MOTOCICLI	12-7
TIPO 50/T2/MT	12-8
TIPO 75/T2 TURISMO LUSSO	12-9
TIPO 125/G.T.S.	12-10
CICLOMOTORI - PRODUZIONE 1959	12-11

NOTE:
These motorcycles were not manufactured or sold by **OFFICINE ALFIERI MASERATI S.P.A.** The Maserati conglomerate was divided between family members in 1952. These vehicles were manufactured and sold by **FABRICA CANDELE ACCUMULATORI MASERATI S.P.A.** This company also made spark plugs, batteries and automotive light bulbs. They had the right to use the Maserati name and Badge for the spark plugs and batteries only. These brochures have been included in this book because they are part of the Maserati History.

Motocicli-Ciclomotori	section 12-1	
TIPO 50/T2		
color sheet	11³/₈ x 8¹/₈" 29 x 20.7 cm	Italian	Style 2B

206

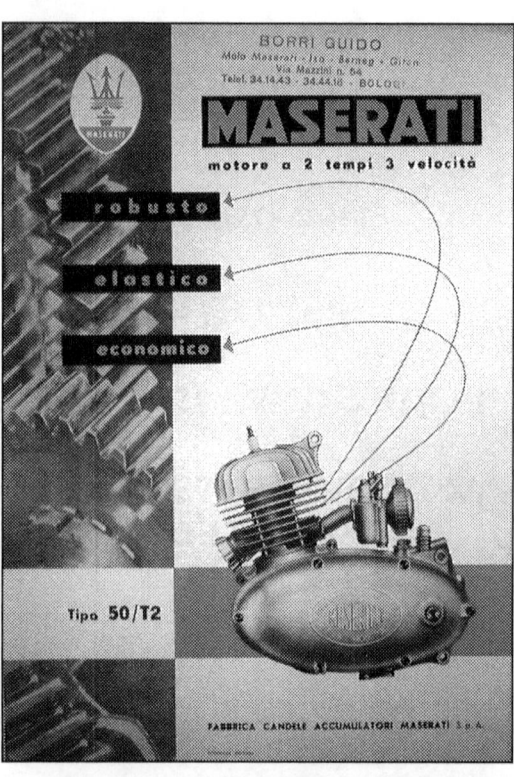

Front:
Background - white
Maserati badge - blue and red on white
Engine and gears - black and white photos
Arrows and stripes behind motor - red
Robusto, elastico , economico - blue on black band
Print - black
Bodoniana Bologna - red

Marked:
Bodoniana Bologna

Rear:
Maserati badge - blue and red
Engine- black and white photo
Maserati - blue on black band
Bottom band - red with black print
Print - black

Motocicli-Ciclomotori			section 12-2		207
L.125/T2, T.V. 125/T2, L.160/T4, 175/S4, 250/T4					
color sheet	12¹³/₁₆ x 8½"	32.4 x 21.8 cm	Italian	Style 2B	

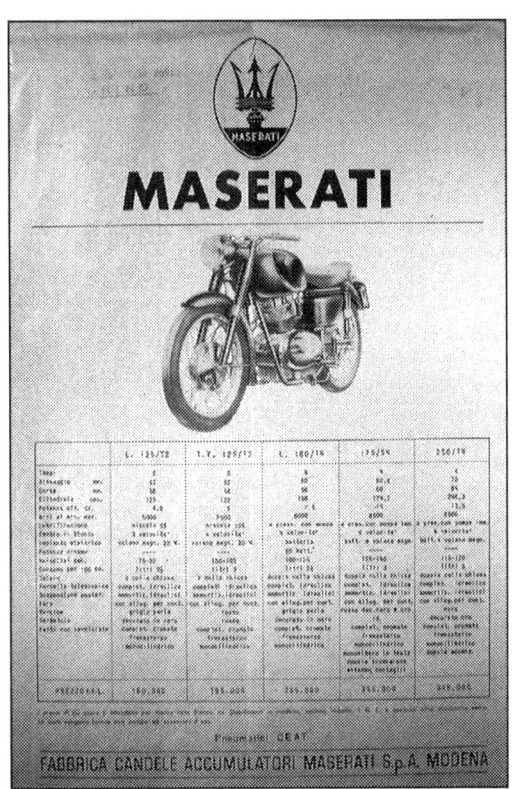

Front:
Background - blue
Print - black

Rear:
Background - blue
Blank

Marked:
None

208	Motocicli-Ciclomotori	section 12-3	
	TIPO 250/T4		
	red sheet	6³/₈ x 8⁵/₈" 16.2 x 22 cm Italian	Style 2A

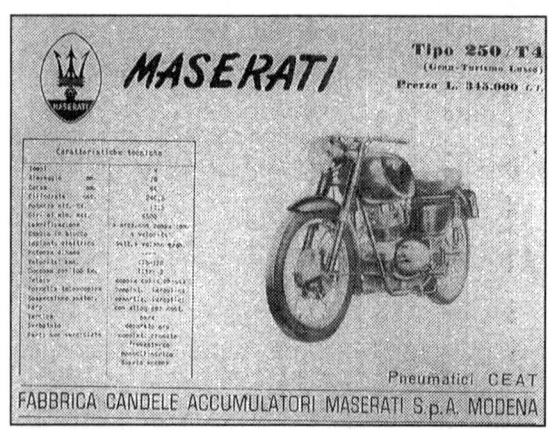

Front:
Background - red
Print - blue

Marked:
None

From the collection of Dr. Adolfo Orsi - Modena, Italy

Motocicli-Ciclomotori			section 12-4	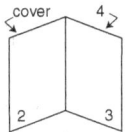
LA TIPO 160/T4, LA TIPO 125/T2				
color folder	6¹¹/₁₆ x 9¹³/₁₆"	17 x 24.9 cm	Italian	Style 1

Cover:
Background - grey green
Maserati badge - black

Page 2:

From the collection of Dr. Adolfo Orsi - Modena, Italy

Motocicli-Ciclomotori

section 12-4

LA TIPO 160/T4, LA TIPO 125/T2

| color folder | 6³/₈ x 8⁵/₈" | 16.2 x 22 cm | Italian | Style 1 |

Page 3:

Page 4:

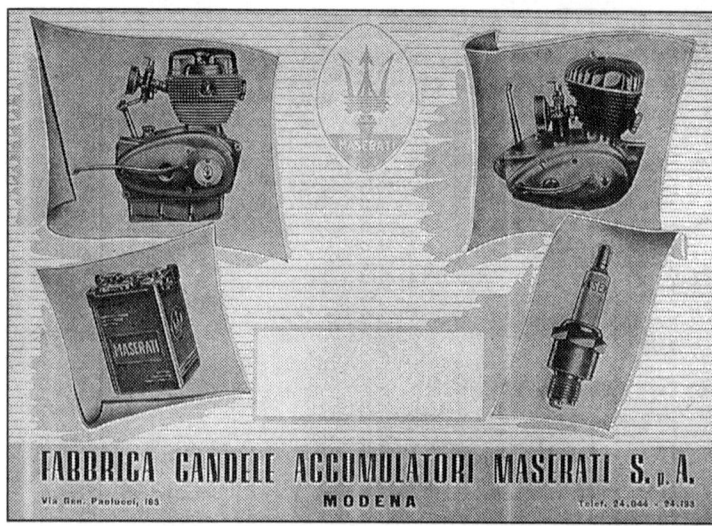

Marked:
STAB. TIP.P.TOSCHI & C. - MODENA

From the collection of Dr. Adolfo Orsi - Modena, Italy

Motocicli-Ciclomotori

MOTO CICLOMOTORI PRODUZIONE 1957

color folder — 8 1/16 x 4 1/4" — 20.5 x 11.4 cm — Italian — Style 4

section 12-5

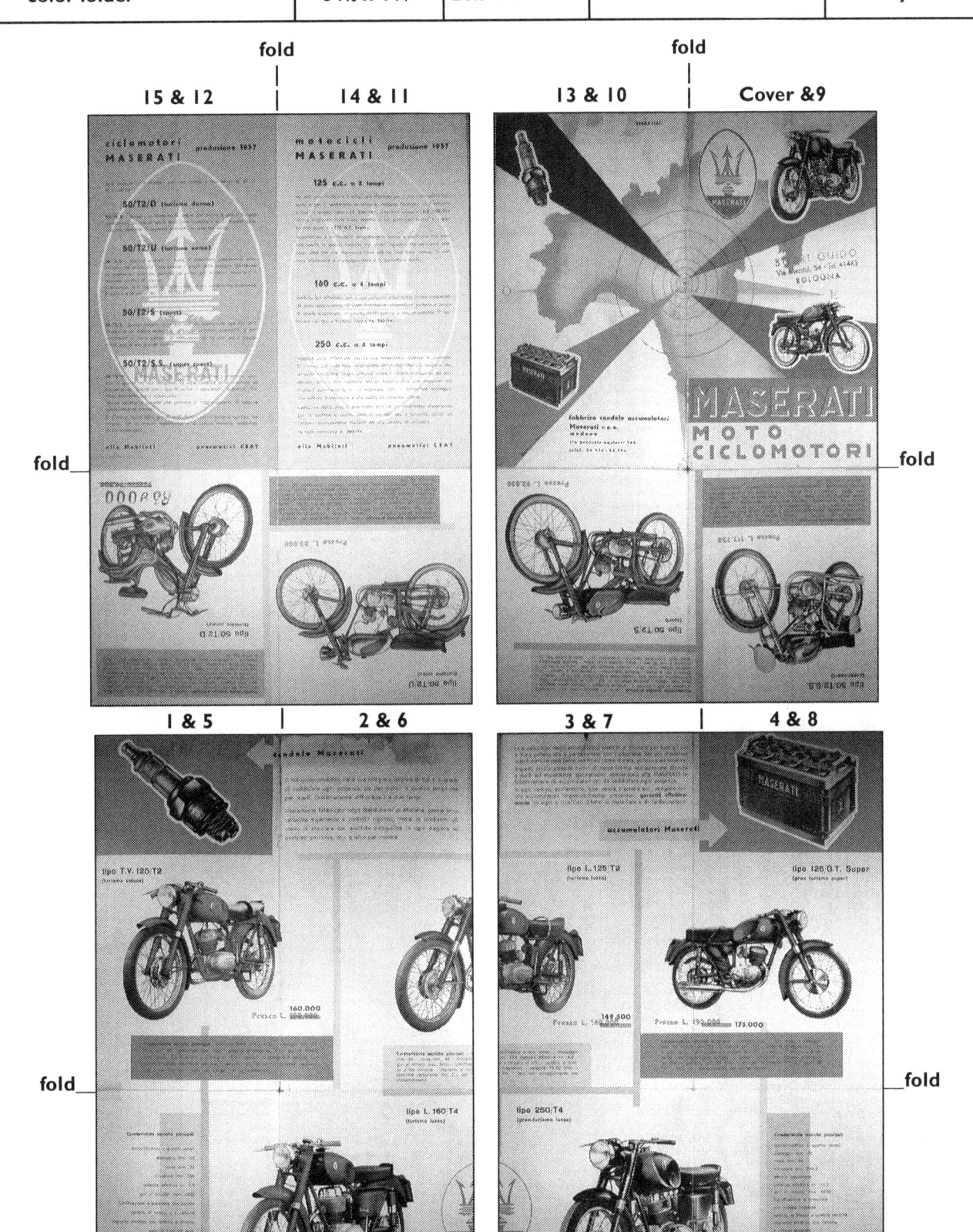

Motocicli-Ciclomotori	section 12-5

MOTO CICLOMOTORI PRODUZIONE 1957

| color folder | 8¹/₁₆ x 4¹/₄" | 20.5 x 11.4 cm | Italian | Style 4 |

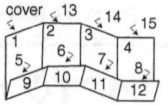

Cover & Page 13 (Rear):
Background - white
Maserati badge - blue and red on white
MASERATI - red on blue Band
MOTO CICLOMOTORI - red on white
Top motorcycle - black on blue triangle
Bottom motorcycle - red on green triangle
Spark plug - steel/rose/gold top on dark brown triangle
Battery - black with orange accents on orange triangle
Italy - yellow with orange shaded edges
MODENA & Corcles - orange
Print - black

Page 1:
Background - white
Spark plug - steel/rose/gold top on blue background
Bike - red
Price - blue
Print - black

Page 2, 3:
Background - white
Motorcycle - red
Print - black
Right vertical band - grey
Bands, arrows, specification band - yellow

Page 4:
Background - white
Battery - black/gold on red background
Specifications - black on red band
Motorcycle - red
Price - blue print
Print - black

Page 5, 6:
Background - white
Specifications - black on yellow
Price - blue print
Vertical stripe - grey
Motorcycle - red
Maserati badge - blue and red
Model type - black print

Page 7, 8:
Background - white
Specifications print - black on grey
Model type - black print
Price - blue print
Vertical stripe - yellow
La prima etc - red

Page 9:
Background - white
Specification print - black on red
Model type - black print
Motorcycle - blue
Vertical stripe - grey
Price - blue print

Page 10:
Background - white
Specification print - black on yellow
Model type - black print
Motorcycle - red
Horizontal Stripe - grey
Price - blue print

Page 11:
Background - white
Specification print - black on red
Model type - black print
Motorcycle - red
Horizontal stripe - yellow
Price - blue print

Page 12:
Background - white
Specification print - black on grey
Model type - black print
Motorcycle - blue
Vertical stripe - yellow
Price - blue print

Page 14:
Background - yellow
Print - black
Maserati badge - white

Page 15:
Background - grey
Print - black
Maserati badge - white
LITOGRAFICA BODONIANA BOLOGNA - blue

Marked:
LITOGRAFICA BODONIANA BOLOGNA

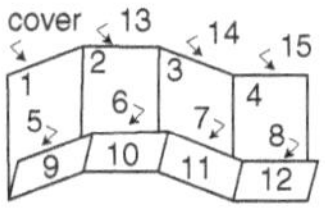

Motocicli-Ciclomotori

MOTOCICLI-CICLOMOTORI PRODUZIONE 1958 (REPRINT)

section 12-6

color sheet original	8¹/₈ x 4¹/₄"	20.7 x 12.1 cm	Italian
color sheet reprint	8 x 4¹⁵/₁₆"	20.4 x 12.5 cm	Style 4

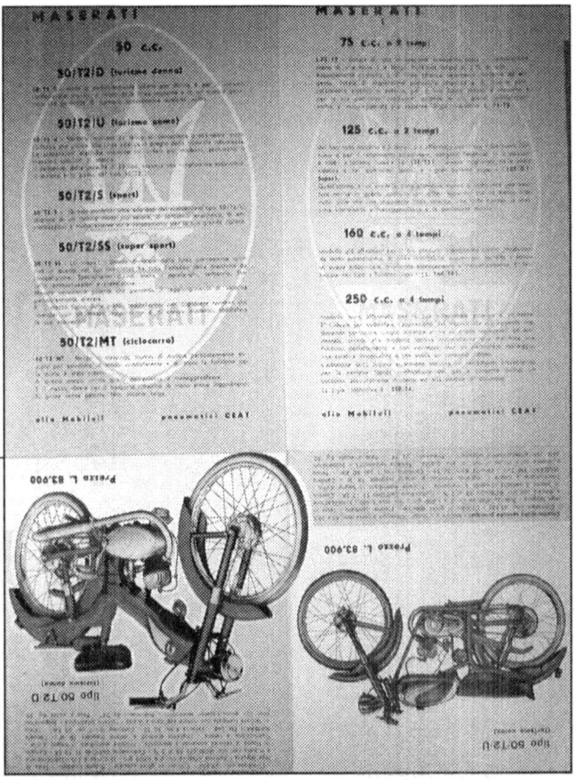

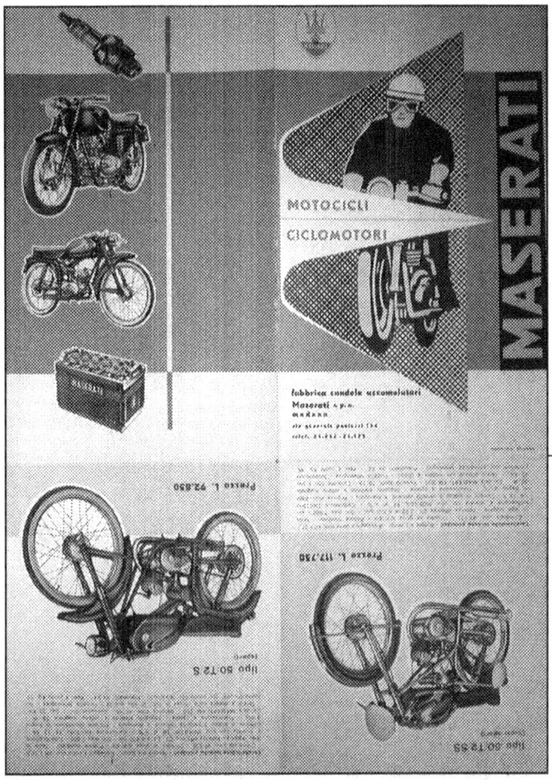

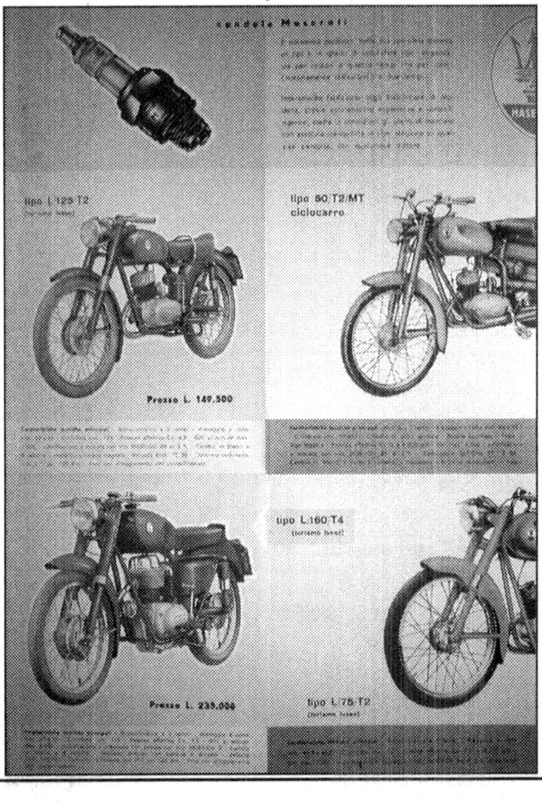

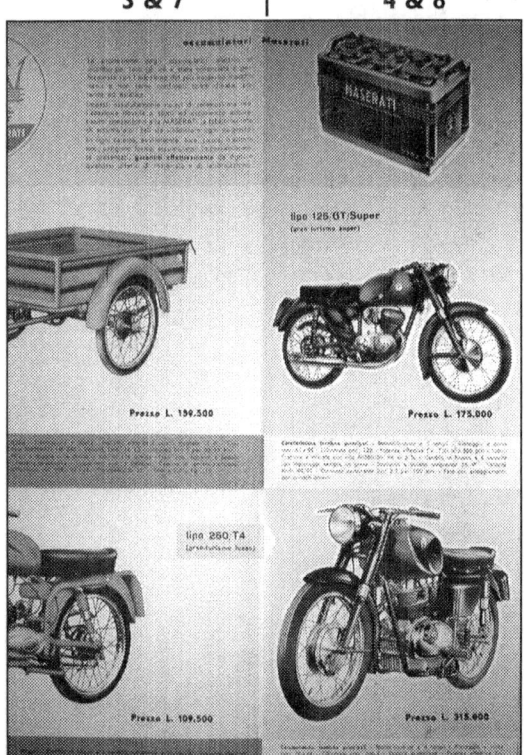

Motocicli-Ciclomotori section 12-6

MOTOCICLI-CICLOMOTORI PRODUZIONE 1958 (REPRINT)

| color sheet original | 8¹/₈ x 4¹/₄" | 20.7 x 12.1 cm | Italian | Style 4 |
| color sheet reprint | 8 x 4¹⁵/₁₆" | 20.4 x 12.5 cm | | |

Cover & Page 13:
Background - white
Maserati badge- blue and red
Maserati - orange on black band
MOTOCICLI / CICLOMOTORI - red
Motorcycle and rider - black with grey highlights
Rider background - yellow/black
Center band - blue
Spark plug - steel / rose / gold top
Top motorcycle - black
Bottom motorcycle - red
Battery - black with orange accents
Print - black

Page 1:
Background: Top - grey
               Center - yellow
               Bottom - white
Print - black
Motorcycle - black
Spark plug - steel / rose / gold top

Page 2, 3:
Background: Top - yellow
               Center - white
               Bottom - blue
Maserati badge - blue and red on white
Print - black
Ciclocarro - grey with blue bands

Page 4:
Background: Top - grey
               Center - yellow
               Bottom - white
Battery - black with orange highlights
Motorcycle - red
Print - black

Page 5:
Background: Top - yellow
               Bottom - white
Motorcycle - red
Print - black

Page 6, 7:
Background: Top - white
               Bottom - blue
Motorcycle - butterscotch
Print - black
Left and right rectangles - yellow

Page 8:
Background: Top - yellow
               Bottom - white
Motorcycle - black with red tank front
Print - black

Page 9:
Background: Top - yellow
               Bottom - white
Motorcycle - blue
Print - black

Page 10:
Background - white
Motorcycle - red
Bottom band- grey
Print - black

Page 11:
Background - white
Motorcycle - red
Bottom band- grey
Print - black

Page 12:
Background: Top - yellow
               Bottom - white
Motorcycle - blue
Print - black

Page 14:
Background - yellow
Print - black
Maserati badge - white

Page 15:
Background - grey
Print - black
Maserati badge - white
Marked:
Bodoniana Bologna

Reprinted and included in:
Le Moto Maserati &
L'artigianato Motociclistico Modernese
By Dante Cardini
Giugno 2002
Marked on front right border Allegato al libro, Le Moto Maserati 2002

Motocicli-Ciclomotori

CANDELE ACCUMULATORI MOTOCICLI

section 12-7

| color folder | 8¼ x 4¾" | 21.1 x 12 cm | ITA, ENG, FRA | Style 4 |

Motocicli-Ciclomotori		section 12-7	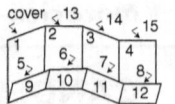
216	**CANDELE ACCUMULATORI MOTOCICLI**		
color folder	8¼ x 4¾"	21.1 x 12 cm	ITA, ENG, FRA	Style 4

Cover & Page 13:
Background - white
Maserati badge- blue and red
Maserati - yellow on black band
Print - black
BODONIANA BOLOGNA - blue
Cartictorature
      Helmet - red/black
      Face - green
      Neck - beige
      Beard - brown
      Scarf - blue
      Body - red
      Tail - red/black
      Bike - red/grey black

Page 1:
Background:
      Top - yellow
      Bottom - white
Motorcycle - red
Print - black

Pages 2, 3:
Background: top - white, bottom - blue
Maserati badge - blue and red
Spark plug - steel/rose/gold top
Battery - black with gold highlights
Cyclewagen - grey with blue bands
Print - black

Page 4:
Background: top - yellow, bottom - white
Motorcycle - red
Print - black

Pages 5, 6:
Background:
      Top - grey
      Center - white
      Bottom - grey
Motorcycle - butterscotch
Print - black on grey

Pages 7, 8:
Motorcycle - black on yellow
Print - black on white
Top band yellow
Bottom band - yellow

Pages 9, 10:
Motorcycle - blue on yellow
Print - black on white
Top - yellow
Bottom - yellow

Pages 11, 12:
Motorcycle - red on white
Top - blue
Bottom - blue
Print - black on blue

Page 14:
Background:
      top - yellow
      bottom - white
Print - black
Motorcycle - blue

Page 15:
Background:
      top - white
      bottom - grey
Motorcycle - red
Print - black

Marked:
BODONIANA BOLOGNA

Motocicli-Ciclomotori			section 12-8		217
TIPO 50/T2/MT					
color sheet	11⁷/₁₆ x 8⅛"	29.2 x 20.6 cm	Italian	Style 2B	

Front:
Backround - yellow with black dots fading to black withyellow dots
Road - white with yellow stripe
Maserati badge - blue and red on white
MASERATI - blue on black band
Motorwagen - grey with blue bands
Print - black
Bottom - blue
BODONIANA BOLOGNA - red

Rear:
Background - white
Maserati badge - blue and red
MASERATI - blue on black band
MOTOCARRO TIPO 50/T2/MT - blue
Print - black
Bottom band - red

Marked: (on front)
BODONIANA BOLOGNA

218	Motocicli-Ciclomotori	section 12-9	
	TIPO 75/T2 TURISMO LUSSO		
	color sheet	11³/₈ x 8¹/₈" 29.0 x 20.5 cm Italian	Style 2B

Front:
Background:
    right - blue
    left - white
Maserati badge - blue and red
MASERATI - blue on black band
Motorcycle - butterscotch on white surrounded by yellow
Rider and bike - black dots
BODONIANA BOLOGNA - red

Rear:
Background - white
Maserati badge - blue and red
MASERATI - blue on black band
Print - black
Bottom band - red
Motorcycle - black and white photo

Marked: (on front)
BODONIANA BOLOGNA

Motocicli-Ciclomotori	section 12-10	
TIPO 125/G.T.S.		219
color sheet / 11½ x 8¼" / 29.2 x 20.8 cm / ITA, ENG, FRA, DEU		Style 2B

Front:
Background - white
Maserati badge - blue and red on white
MASERATI - blue on black band
Motorcycle - red on white
Top/Bottom band - grey
Top cresent:
    left - yellow
    right - red
Bottom cresent:
    left - white
    right - red
Right vertical bands right to left: red, yellow, blue, yellow
Print - black

Rear:
Background - white
Maserati badge - blue and red
MASERATI - black on blue band
Top heading - red
Stripes - red
Print - black

Marked: (on rear)
TIP. MANTOVANI - MODENA

Motocicli-Ciclomotori

220 — section 12-11

CICLOMOTORI - PRODUZIONE 1959

| black and orange sheet | 12½ x 8⅝" | 32 x 22 cm | Italian | Style 2B |

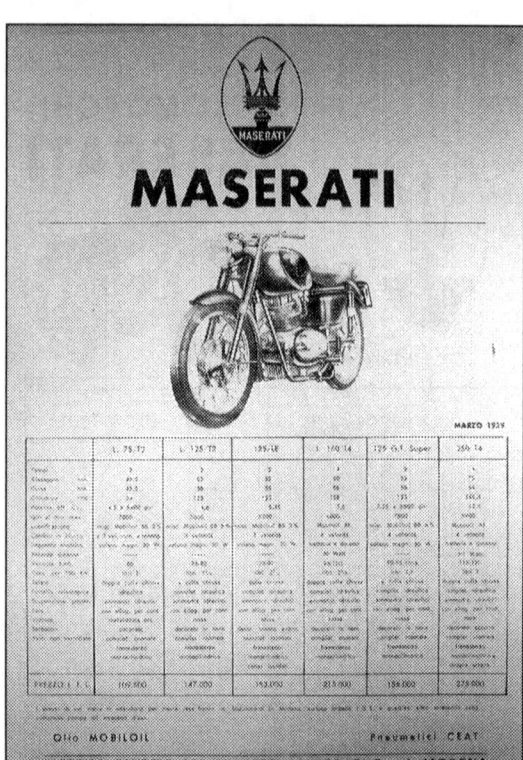

Front:
Background - orange
Print - black

Rear:
Background - orange
Print - black

Marked:
None

From the collection of Dr. Adolfo Orsi - Modena, Italy

NOTES

NOTES

www.ingramcontent.com/pod-product-compliance
Lightning Source LLC
Chambersburg PA
CBHW060249240426
43673CB00047B/1898